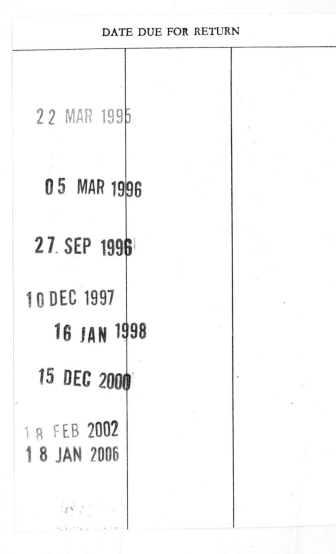

REFORM AND REACTION

THE POLITICO-RELIGIOUS
BACKGROUND OF THE
SPANISH CIVIL WAR

CHAPEL HILL
THE UNIVERSITY OF
NORTH CAROLINA PRESS

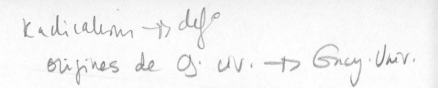

REFORM
AND
REACTION

p. 39

BY JOSÉ M. SÁNCHEZ

For Carol

PREFACE

The study of church-state relations in modern Spanish history is an extremely complex but nonetheless fascinating task. It is also frustrating, for it offers no answers or solutions to the problems it poses. One would hope that here, certainly, a detailed study of one of the most crucial periods in politico-ecclesiastical relations could profitably be applied to prevent future conflicts. Unfortunately, my hopes are not great, for if nothing else, the history of Spain bears out the dictum that man never profits from experience: he merely learns to predict his next mistake.

For those nurtured in the Western liberal tradition, the Spanish situation would appear to be the result of a failure to heed the lessons of the nineteenth century: church and state should have been separated as in the other Western nations; then Spain would have progressed as they did. This "solution" simply begs the question. Catholicism and the church have been intimately connected with the lives of all Spaniards since the middle ages. The church has been and is a powerful institution. The profundity of the Catholic tradition in Spain can be almost incomprehensible to non-Spaniards. Where else, for example, could a historian write of this intimacy between church and nation as did Marcelino Menéndez y Pelayo in his fiery challenging enunciation: "Spain! evangelist to half the world; Spain! hammer of heretics, light of Trent, sword of Rome, cradle of Saint Ignatius . . . ; this is our greatness and unity: we have no other."

The Spanish church is and always has been a state within a state; this condition, in fact, is true of all churches in all states. Only in totalitarian states does "separation" have any meaning, and it is in such states that the free exercise of religion is crushed. This is not to suggest that the solution to the Spanish politico-religious problem can be found in impractical sixteenth-century concepts. But neither should we assume that the atomistic nineteenth-century liberal approach to church-state conflicts has eternal verity, or is even valid today. Churches always exert moral, cultural, and intellectual influences upon people and it is a narrow mind that would hold that man is solely a political creature. Man has many more needs than political ones, and he cannot be separated into compartments. Churches do influence men, and for the faithful, rightly so; for them, salvation is man's most important aim.

Hence the conflict. To propose a solution to the Spanish politico-religious problem would be impertinent if not impossible, nor is it the historian's task. I would only hope that this study can do what all histories should: not predict, not preach, not censure, but enlighten.

Portions of this book have appeared in article form

in *Church History* (December, 1962) and in *The Catholic Historical Review* (April, 1963).

I would like to express my appreciation to the many persons who made this study possible: in Spain, Dr. José Ibáñez Cerdá and the staff of the Biblioteca Nacional, the staff of the Hemeroteca Municipal in Madrid, Don José Luís Vásquez-Dodero, and Don Rodolfo Núñez de las Cuevas; in the United States, Dr. E. Taylor Parks of the Historical Division of the State Department, the staff of the National Archives, and Dr. Howard Cline and the staff of the Hispanic Foundation of the Library of Congress. I profited greatly from conversations with Professors Juan José Linz of Columbia University and the late Willard A. Smith of the University of Toledo. I owe a special debt of gratitude to the Social Science Research Council for a predoctoral fellowship that enabled me and my family to spend a year in Spain, and to the Ford Foundation for a grant under its program for assisting American university presses in the publication of works in the humanities and the social sciences. Finally, I am extremely grateful to my former mentors at the University of New Mexico, Professors Miguel Jorrín, France V. Scholes, and above all to Professor Edwin Lieuwen, without whose encouragement, criticism, and aid this study would never have been written.

José M. Sánchez

Saint Louis University
May, 1963

CONTENTS

REFORM AND REACTION

"We have declared for the Republic. What shall we do with the priest?" (Message received by the home ministry in Madrid from the mayor of a small Spanish town, April 15, 1931.)

CHAPTER 1

THE QUESTION

On the night of July 19, 1936, dense clouds of pungent smoke hung over most of the cities of Spain. The churches of Spain were burning. Earlier that morning the army garrisons all over the peninsula had raised the standard of rebellion against the government of the Second Spanish Republic. All day long Spaniards loyal to the republic had battled the rebellious military, and now, in the late evening, the mobs attacked the churches.

Any Spaniard of even moderately liberal opinion could spell out the reason for the burnings: Spain was simply in the throes of another political upheaval. Revolutions, *coups d'état, pronunciamientos*—the political history of Spain for over a century—were always accompanied by church burnings. The church, he would say, had always meddled in politics. It had always allied itself with the plutocrats, the landlords, and the oligarchy. Therefore, it should, and did, expect a ritual purification by fire whenever the people of Spain took justice into their own hands.

There were, however, other events occurring that same evening which the anticlerical Spaniard could not shrug off as "Spanish tradition." As the sun set, trucks and busses drew up to the doors of monasteries, rectories, and convents. Priests, monks, nuns, and seminarians were forced out of their residences and into the vehicles; they were then transported into a night of terror. Most were taken to the nearest anarchist headquarters where they were tried and sentenced, all in a few moments, for "crimes against the people." Some were carted off to prison. Others were driven to the outskirts of town, or in the larger cities, to a quiet spot in the park. There, dismounted, they were tied together. Some of the clerics begged for mercy; others stood heroically unmoved, praying silently. All—cowards, martyrs, and confused—faced their executioners until the fusillade snuffed out their lives.

Similar scenes occurred all over republican-held Spain for the next few months, until by January, 1937, the revolutionary fury spent itself. In those six months almost seven thousand priests, monks, seminarians, and nuns were killed.[1] Practically every church in Loyalist Spain was in ruins. Never had the Spanish church seen such a prodigious bloodletting.

Why?

The answer to this question is not academic. Millions of persons staked their lives and hundreds of thousands died for what they believed to be the true answer. The Spanish bishops, in a pastoral letter of September, 1937, called upon all Spanish Catholics to support General Francisco Franco's Nationalist forces because, they

1. Thirteen bishops, 4,171 secular clerics, 2,265 monks, and 283 nuns is the most reliable estimate in Antonio Montero Moreno, *Historia de la persecución religiosa en España, 1936-1939* (Madrid, 1961), p. 762.

claimed, the church had suffered from persecution at the hands of republicans ever since the Second Republic came into being in 1931.[2] Their appeal was heard abroad and Catholics in every land offered prayers and donations for the Nationalist cause. Likewise, the republicans appealed for all Spaniards to join them against an unholy triumvirate—landlords, officers, and priests—that had conspired to defraud the Spanish people of their birthright to self-government and social justice. This appeal was also heard abroad, as millions donated and thousands joined the international brigades to fight in Spain.

Spaniards and foreigners took up arms and fought out the issues. Political pamphlets explained all in simple terms during the Civil War years. Few persons made an honest attempt to approach problems objectively; everything was done to arouse passions, either for or against the republic. There were no middle positions. Either the church was all right or all wrong. Either the republic was a democracy fighting against an oligarchic fascism, or General Franco was a new Saviour bringing order and Christianity to land governed by an anarchic Bolshevist government.

On that April morning of 1939 when the Nationalist troops marched into Madrid—that same morning which found thousands of disappointed Loyalists withering away their lives in French refugee camps—the Civil War was ended. But, it did not settle the politico-religious problem, much less offer any solution to it.

The questions remain. Why were the churches burned? Why were the clergy killed? Why did an institution devoted to man's salvation find itself persecuted by those who also sought man's deliverance from evil?

2. The letter is in *The New York Times*, September 3, 1937.

CHAPTER 2

THE SEEDS
OF CONFLICT

In the year 391 A.D., Theodosius, Emperor of Rome, issued a decree which established Christianity as the religion of the empire. In the westernmost part of the empire, the Iberian peninsula, the union of church and state officially came into being. Nothing about this conjunction distinguished the Spanish union as essentially different from that in other parts of the empire.

When the peninsula was overrun by Germanic barbarians in the fifth and sixth centuries, the Spanish church transferred its allegiance to the new Visigothic rulers. Although the earlier Visigothic kings were Arian heretics, orthodoxy ultimately prevailed, and the two jurisdictions continued to be united in purpose and policy. However, significant changes were taking place in the union. For one thing, the monarchy was beset by fratricidal struggles, and in its weakened condition it allowed the church, at the Council of Toledo of 633, to establish the privilege of episcopal coronation of the kings—a privilege tantamount to clerical control of the monarchy. Furthermore, at this time there occurred in Spain a process that was taking place in every other land: the church took on the national characteristics of the people.

In 711, internal squabbles among the Visigothic nobility culminated in an invitation from one of the warring factions to the Moslems in Africa to help them. The Moslems crossed the Straits of Gibraltar—and helped themselves. Within eight years they had overrun almost the entire peninsula and had reached the Pyrenees. The followers of Mohammed established a new state in Spain, and later, seceding from the central Moslem government, they founded the Independent Caliphate of Córdoba, surely the brightest light of civilization in western Europe. The Moslems were tolerant in their relations with the conquered Spanish Christians and allowed them freedom of worship, but there is no doubt that the non-Moslems labored under civil disabilities, especially as the caliphate grew weaker.

What the Moslems had conquered in eight years, it was to take the Christians eight centuries to reconquer. In the mountainous areas of northwest Spain, some of the Visigothic nobility still held out against the Moslems. They formed the nucleus of the new Christian kingdoms of Spain. These groups found a natural ally in the church, for it heartily endorsed their *reconquista,* obviously for reasons of religious orthodoxy, but also because the church desired political power in an age when the church sought supremacy throughout Europe. It was during these years that a definite characteristic of both the Spanish people and the Spanish church was formed—a militant crusading intolerance which demanded the extirpation of religious heterodoxy.

In 1492, Ferdinand and Isabella, the united monarchs of Aragón and Castile, perfected the technique of fusing religious fervor and national patriotism and completely crushed the last remnants of Moslem rule in Spain. But the militant spirit developed for over eight hundred years could not be subdued once the Moslems were gone.

Ferdinand and Isabella, the Catholic Kings, channeled off some of this crusading spirit to effect the conquest of America, but they wisely used that which remained to effect political unity at home. For, if Spain was united in their persons it remained separated in reality. They made the church a most effective instrument of unity; the institution was Spain's only common denominator. Although the church had preserved much of its independence from royal control before 1479, the Catholic Kings initiated a policy of domination over it, and their sixteenth-century successors successfully completed the task. For example, the Inquisition was re-established in Spain, this time under complete crown control in a royal effort to stamp out religious heresy and political liberty.

The papacy of the fifteenth and sixteenth centuries recognized the Spanish crown's aims of religious unity; the popes also realized that the vast missionary program of converting a new world needed the monarchs' support and guidance. To these ends, they granted the Spanish crown a series of *de facto* concessions known as the *patronato real* (royal patronage). In effect, these concessions gave the crown the right to nominate members of the church hierarchy in some parts of Spain and the right of appointment in other parts (and in the entire New World). The monarchs were also granted the privilege of collecting some of the church revenues. These powers proved so effective that later monarchs sought to extend them to include all of the higher clerical appointments in the nation.[1]

Despite the broad powers granted in the *patronato*, it did not mean that the crown had come to complete terms with the papacy. The sixteenth century saw many a struggle between Rome and Spain, and both Charles V and Philip II tightened their control over the Spanish church, assuring themselves of the support of the Spanish clergy for their often antipapal policies. While many Spanish clerics supported their monarchs, others realized the threat to the church's independence and sought to counter royal absolutism. This church-state struggle might have become violent had it not been for events in other countries which served to channel off some of this factious energy, for this was the century of the Protestant Revolt. Because the Catholic Kings had started to weed out corruption twenty years before Martin Luther began his revolt against Rome, and because the crown had been successful in its policy of enforcing religious unity, Protestantism never established itself in Spain. Instead, Spain formed the bulwark of Catholic reaction and under Philip II led the crusade to re-establish unity of faith in Europe. Despite the Prudent King's failures abroad, he effectively welded militant Catholicism to Spanish nationalism within the country. As a result, the incipient church-state struggle was submerged for a time. Another important result was that Spain did not come to enjoy the religious toleration that was a practical consequence of the civil wars of religion in other countries.

But the international struggle, the drive towards national religious unity, and the identification of Spanish

1. See W. Eugene Shiels, S. J., *King and Church: The Rise and Fall of the Patronato Real* (Chicago, 1961) for a penetrating study of this power.

nationalism with Catholicism also helped to give the Spanish church its greatest moment of glory. It produced a remarkable breed of cleric during that querulous age. The greatest intellectuals of Spain—indeed of the Catholic world—were churchmen. They dominated the Council of Trent. They wrote scholarly treatises on natural law, theology, history, almost every facet of learning. Moreover, many of them were strong advocates of individual rights against royal absolutism. Such clerics as Francisco de Vittoria and Francisco Suárez, for example, defended Spaniards against the transgressions of their monarchs. As a result of all these factors, the Spanish church achieved cultural and intellectual pre-eminence over all other institutions in Spain, although it still labored under the crown's political domination.

At the same time, a Spanish nobleman named Ignatio de Loyola evinced his organizational skill and founded the Society of Jesus. It rapidly became the most militant body within the church, and its influence was felt throughout the world. Fervently ultramontane at its inception, it posed a threat to the Spanish crown and was opposed by both Charles V and Philip II, until the latter, in a rare act of political wisdom, sent the Jesuits to expend their energies on foreign missions and education throughout the vast colonial empire.

In spite of the energy of the crown, the church, and the Spanish people, by the beginning of the seventeenth century decay had begun to set in. Spain's intellectual, political, and cultural renaissance had come to an end. Never had an empire risen and fallen so spectacularly. A complete evaluation of the causes of decline is too lengthy for this survey, but much of the weakness could be attributed to a combination of poor rulers, inflationary fiscal policies, and social stagnation. In this situation the ruling classes became corrupt. The church followed suit, and many of the clergy were content to rely on the merits of their predecessors; there appeared a notable loss of zeal. Furthermore, the church-state union had become so solidified and the monolithic character of the church so impervious to change, that it could not provide capable leadership in this time of crisis. The church suffered as the nation suffered.

In 1700, the decline of Spain reached its nadir. In that year, the imbecilic and impotent Charles II, last of the Spanish Hapsburgs, died without issue. Succession to the throne led to war between French Bourbons and Austrian Hapsburgs, until the settlement of Utrecht in 1713 recognized a Bourbon, Philip V, as king of Spain.

Under the Bourbons, Spain pulled out of its slump. Spaniards also witnessed the birth of a new era of statecraft, for not even the most absolutist of the Hapsburgs had ever enunciated or practiced the Bourbon concept of *l'état ce moi*. The Spanish church was wary of Bourbon centralism, but the papacy gave the crown unlimited patronage in 1763; less than four years later Charles III gave life to the principle by expelling the Jesuits from the Spanish Empire. Charles III also began the spoliation of church property, through the device of limiting the size of the religious orders and confiscating the unused lands. There was reason to Charles' policy, for the church was the greatest landowner in the nation, and Charles sincerely desired agrarian reform. To counter the crown, the clergy espoused the cause of regional separatism and led the fight against the enlightened despotism of the Bourbons. As a result, the vital element of the church was continuously at war with the Bourbons—although, by and large, the crown still controlled the episcopate.

By the beginning of the nineteenth century, the Spanish church had experienced almost fifteen centuries of union with the Christian kings of Spain. The Catholic tradition had imparted much to Spain—national unity, intellectual and cultural greatness—and the state had protected the church and fomented its aims. But, since the fifteenth century, the church's relationship with the state had been one of conflict within union, and conflict now outweighed harmony. Few Spaniards wanted the state to cease its benevolent attitude toward the church, but then few Spaniards realized that the traditional harmony had by 1800 become more apparent than real.

With this background of conflict within union, both the church and the crown faced the nineteenth century. Both institutions stood in dire need of reform; neither was prepared to face the vicissitudes of the future.

A new world was on the horizon, a world that was to bring to fruition the ideas of Rousseau—ideas that would trigger the chain of events leading from liberalism through socialism to fascism. The rise of the masses to political and social power would try the resources of both church and state to lead the proletariat to a nonviolent solution of its problems. In this instance, both jurisdictions were to be found wanting. It was against this background that the struggles of nineteenth- and twentieth-century Spain were to be enacted.

lit: se trouver en défaut.

CHAPTER 3

LIBERALISM AND CARLISM

The nineteenth century descended with a shock upon Spain in 1808. In that watershed year of Spanish history, an enraged nation took up arms against a Napoleonic army that had taken their king from them. The French proclaimed Napoleon Bonaparte's brother, Joseph, as the new King of Spain, but only a small group of enlightened and opportunist *afrancescados* accepted the new monarch; the rest of the Spanish nation fought a savage war against the hated Frenchman and his armies.

While Spaniards fought for the return of their monarch, Ferdinand VII, the very absence of their king led directly to the struggles that were to shape the nineteenth century. In that chaos called Spain, the state had simply disappeared. The government no longer functioned. Two institutions—the army and the church—quickly stepped in to fill the governmental void, and they became the protagonists of the century's struggle.

The Spanish army, long the scorn of Europe's milita-
rists, displayed its weakness by losing battle after battle to
the French; but in that debility it found strength—a reformation as it were—for the troops turned to guerrilla warfare, in which action they were supported by many non-
professionals. In conjunction with Wellington's British
regulars they drove the Napoleonic army out of the peninsula, and in the process a new Spanish Army emerged,
formed of the remnants of the old army and the guerrillas.
This force now tasted glory, as had Spanish armies of the
sixteenth century, and it wanted more.

The Spanish church, in one of its greatest moments of
glory, rallied the people to the defense of their nation. It
roused national aspirations as it had done during the days
of the *reconquista*. Church leaders also saw an opportunity to take advantage of the governmental void. Having
experienced centuries of domination by the state, they
now planned to make themselves so powerful that the
secular jurisdiction would never again encroach upon
their rights and privileges. But the church, unlike the
army, did not experience a reformation—in the same way
that the guerrillas reformed the army—and it could not
cope with the power it sought. It made the mistake not
of seeking political power to avoid domination in the
future but of being unable to use that power for the bene-
fit of the entire nation.

The opposing forces of the nineteenth century were
formulated; they needed only the ideology of circumstances to give them life.

i

Four years after the war against the French had
begun, in the southern seaport town of Cádiz a representative Cortes met to formulate a plan of government

in the king's absence. The Cortes members were from the towns along the eastern seaboard, mainly because the French still held the inland lines of transportation. Because these politicians represented predominantly commercial and mercantile areas, they brought with them a new political ideology—liberalism. And, in that same year, they founded the Spanish Liberal party.

The Spanish Liberals—who gave the word *liberalismo* to the world—had received much of the initial impetus for their ideas from the Bourbons' enlightened despotism, and later, from the French revolutionaries. Basically, their governmental philosophy was derived from their economic ideology of *laissez faire;* they stressed the idea of freedom from restraint.

The Liberals' political aspirations found expression in a desire for constitutional government and civil liberties. Being secularists, rationalists, and optimists, they opposed any form of religious influence in governmental affairs and any interference of the church in worldly activities. This view was, of course, directly opposed to the aims of the Spanish church in that year of 1812.

The Liberals' religious policy was aimed at eliminating the church's political power, by decreasing its economic and educational influence. Thus, they directed their ambitions towards disentailing church lands (for the church's wealth in 1812 was land) and replacing religious education with secular education. Both of these tasks were difficult, for the church was strong. As a result of both the power of the church and the inherent weakness of Spanish liberalism, the Spanish Liberals became more doctrinaire and idealistic than Liberals in other European countries. They felt that they could make no gains, complete no reforms, as long as the church retained its power and strength. They became obsessed with the struggle against the church, and even in later years when the church had lost its strength, the Liberals still singled out the church as their main enemy. Spanish liberalism became completely identified with anticlericalism, so much so that anticlericalism often became the only distinguishing characteristic of the Spanish Liberal.

What was the essence of their anticlericalism? Anticlericalism, basically, is a feeling directed against the clergy and the church, as an institution, particularly against their political role. In other words, there is no anticlericalism without clericalism—the main tenet of clericalism being that the clergy have the obligation to direct the faithful in all of their duties, even in those unrelated in any way to spiritual ends. Both radical clericalism and radical anticlericalism are based on fallacies: the anticlerical contends that the material and spiritual realms are completely separate and that the church has no right to instruct the faithful except in their patently religious duties; while the clerical holds that the spiritual and material orders are so closely intertwined that one's salvation hinges directly upon every judgment he makes —even on clearly nonspiritual choices, such as forms of government. Thus, the inherent danger in anticlericalism is that of completely divorcing religion from reality, while clericalism is dangerous because it restricts individual freedom in those areas in which the clergy have no right to do so.

Spanish anticlericalism was usually more violent than that in other lands because clericalism was stronger in Spain, and because Spaniards in modern times usually tended to violent solutions of their problems. It cannot be denied that the clergy were often the scapegoats of mob violence, simply because they were easy to locate and usually offered little resistance. Alejandro Lerroux, a lifelong anticlerical, succinctly summed it up: "The mob knows that Christ will not come down off the Cross to fire a machine-gun."[1]

It is important to note that although anticlericals showed a lack of respect for the clergy, they were not necessarily disrespectful of religion. Indeed, many anticlericals justified their actions by claiming a deeper respect for religion on the grounds that they wanted to purify the church by ridding it of an unworthy element.

The Spanish Liberals of 1812, fired by this anticlericalism, intended to deprive the church of its political and economic power. They drafted the first constitution in Spanish history and based it on the principle that sovereignty resided in the people. Although they attempted to gain church support by declaring Catholicism to be the established religion (and the only religion tolerated) —for, in all justice to the Liberals, they were Catholics— theirs was an anticlerical document. The constitution of 1812 limited the size of all *conventos* (residences of the regular clergy) to no more than twelve members and provided that the unused lands and buildings be appropriated by the government. It also provided for the abolition of the inquisition.

The constitution completed, however, was not the constitution enacted, and when the Liberals set about the task of putting their constitution in practice, they revealed an inherent weakness in Spanish liberalism. By its nature, liberalism required a flourishing economy, an industrial revolution, and a large-sized middle class to take advantage of the Liberal reforms; free trade, free thought, and constitutional government meant nothing to the peasant or day-laborer. The Spanish economy sim-

1. *La pequeña historia: Apuntes para la historia grande vividos y redactados por el autor* (Buenos Aires, 1945), p. 32.

ply could not furnish these elements. Spanish liberalism, as an ideology, was stifled from the beginning by the lack of a dynamic vehicle. Instead, the army drifted to its banner, and the movement was crippled at birth by those twins of ill fortune—a weak economy and an overweening army.

In 1814, Ferdinand VII—El Deseado (The Desired One)—returned to Spain; never has desire gone so unfulfilled. The king knew that he had to make a choice: either the army or the church would have to be the mainstay of his regime. Because the church was the stronger of the two, and because the army was joining the Liberal camp, he chose the church. With the support of the church, which was determined now to assert its will over the monarch and to eradicate liberalism, Ferdinand abolished the 1812 constitution and inaugurated nineteen years of complete despotism. Church and crown became inseparably united in tyranny. There can be little wonder that the Liberals now became more entrenched in their anticlericalism and emboldened in their desire to do away with the church's power and influence.

The Liberals turned to a secret organization—Freemasonry—as the vehicle for their aims. Freemasonry had been founded in Spain by the English in 1728, and until 1808, it remained an enlightened society to which almost all of the Bourbon ministers belonged. It was a relatively harmless organization at first. When the French invaded Spain, they brought in the radical Grand Oriente lodges, and these became useful meeting places for Liberal politicians and army officers. Indeed, one of the reasons why the Liberals abolished the inquisition in 1812 had been the latter's ability to ferret out the Freemasonic lodges.

As a result of the regime's persecution of the Liberals after 1814—and it was a harsh repression—Freemasonry became almost completely identified with Spanish liberalism; in this manner liberalism was transformed from a movement into a secret sect and it never gained the support of the masses. However, Freemasonry played an important role in the early years of the Liberal party, although—and despite the pronouncements of Spanish clerics—it never had much effect thereafter.[2]

By 1820, when the Liberals decided to rise against the monarch, Spanish liberalism appeared to be a seed on barren ground; it was already solidly doctrinaire, sterile, sectarian, and above all, lacking in that dynamic impulse that characterized liberalism in other countries.

ii

In 1820, in that same town of Cádiz which had witnessed the birth of the constitution, thousands of troops waited to embark for America to effect the reconquest of the Spanish Empire. Among the milling, dissatisfied soldiers, an officer named Rafael Riego raised the standard of rebellion against Ferdinand VII and proclaimed the constitution of 1812. The movement gathered momentum, and Ferdinand was forced to promise his allegiance to the constitution. In the chaotic three years that followed, governments alternated among many Liberal groups and the nation was once again thrown into con-

2. The influence of the lodges declined after the Liberals had achieved their aims in the defeat of the Carlists, and they became simple clubs, especially after the working class movements became the centers of radicalism. Because of their secrecy and distribution they have remained as convenient meeting places for those opposed to any non-liberal regime. But, it seems obvious that the lodges served more as vehicles for liberal ideas rather than as sources of motivation. Even after the radicalism of the Socialists and Anarchists far surpassed any Masonic radicalism, the lodges remained and are, today, the great *bête noire* of the Spanish church. See Gerald Brenan, *The Spanish Labyrinth: An Account of the Social and Political Background of the Civil War* (Cambridge, 1950), pp. 206-8, 234.

RADICALISM

fusion. The Concert of Europe kept a close eye on Spain, heard Ferdinand's appeals for a restoration to absolutism, and in 1823 sent a French armed force to put an end to this first Liberal interlude.

Although the Concert favored a restoration, it had not looked kindly upon Ferdinand's tyrannical rule, for despotic governments were open invitations to radicalism and liberalism. Therefore, one of the conditions of his restoration was that the inquisition remain dissolved. Ferdinand was forced to agree. The more reactionary elements in Spain viewed this concession as proof that their monarch was drifting toward liberalism; furthermore, the clergy among them saw that the church could never be safe unless they had a monarch of their own choosing, one who would be completely answerable to them. This group came to oppose both Ferdinand and the Liberals; they were the founders of Carlism.

The Carlists had deep roots in Spain, although they did not find a name for their ideology until 1833. There had always been Spaniards who had favored some form of theocracy in which the church's power would be supreme over the state's. In an immediately practical sense, there was some reason to their contention; after all, the state had not done so well for the last two centuries and there were many clerics willing to try their hand at government. These Spaniards desired an intimate union of church and monarchy, tempered of course by the restraints of the natural law, but nonetheless with the church retaining sweeping powers.

At first, Carlism was no more than a reactionary political movement, akin to many others in post-Napoleonic Europe. It was a natural occurrence that there should be a reaction to the decade of political chaos under the Liberals and Ferdinand—for make no mistake, Ferdinand was not a conservative; he was a corrupt tyrant. But in Spain, reaction had a firm basis. During the preceding century agrarian and pastoral interests, especially in northern Spain, had crystallized feeling against the centralizing, mercantilistic policies of the eighteenth-century Bourbons. This movement also aroused the sympathy of the separatist movements in the Basque and Catalan provinces. Thus, by the nineteenth century, Carlism came to oppose everything that liberalism stood for: it was agrarian, clerical, rural, separatist, and basically feudal, while the Liberals were centralist, urban, commercial, and anticlerical. Carlism attracted widespread support in Spain because of the nation's basically agrarian character, but, unfortunately for the Carlists, they became tied up with a dynastic struggle.

In 1833 Ferdinand died. His heir was a two-year old daughter, Isabella II, and as a consequence of her minor age, her mother, María Cristina, ruled as regent. María Cristina was not a strong woman, and she had a decided penchant for army officers—a move toward liberalism as the Carlists saw it, although they had opposed the extension of the dynasty through Isabella long before Ferdinand's death. The Carlists had their own candidate for the throne, a pliable man who had their same absolutist views and who could be made to conform to their wishes. This was Ferdinand's brother, Carlos. The Carlists contended that the throne of Spain could not pass to a woman, for this was a violation of the Salic law that had been promulgated by the Bourbon Philip V in 1713. Although Charles IV had abrogated this decree, he had done so in secret, and therefore the Carlists claimed the abrogation was not valid. In any event, this dynastic struggle was not the cause but merely a symptom of

Carlism, which would have been a strong movement had there been no struggle for the throne.

María Cristina, faced with the Carlist threat and demands that she turn over the regency to her brother-in-law, was forced to rely upon the Liberals for support. She made concessions in the form of a constitution, the Royal Statute of 1834. The statute was a conservative document; it retained Catholicism as the state religion with all of its rights and privileges and allowed no religious toleration. Nothing shows the character of the Carlists more clearly than their rejection of this document, for it proved that they did not want official privileges for the church but rather domination over the country; in other words, although they made much of the rights of religion, these were not paramount in their program. In 1834, war broke out between the Liberals and the Carlists. Fighting raged throughout Vasconia and Catalonia.

An interesting and foreboding incident occurred in Madrid in the first year of the war. There was a severe cholera epidemic in the Spanish capital that year, and the rumor was spread that the Jesuits had been poisoning the wells. A mob attacked the Jesuit churches, burned them, and killed some one hundred Jesuits. This event is significant, for the people who attacked the Jesuits in this first violent display of anticlericalism in Spain were not Liberals; they were the people of Madrid, the urban working classes. As most of the Jesuits were Carlists, the attack was an indication that the urban masses were not in sympathy with the clergy's political role.

By 1835, liberalism and Carlism had come to polarize politics in Spain. Henceforth, the Liberals became more anticlerical, more idealistic, more doctrinaire, and more utopian; the Carlists became more reactionary, more fanatical, more fixed in their desire to turn back the clock.

desamortización

An impasse was reached which threatened to produce an even more violent and prolonged civil war. That it did not is attributed to the activities of Juan Álvarez Mendizábal, the new Liberal prime minister, who in 1835 confiscated all of the church's lands and put them up for public sale. This *desamortización* had profound and unforeseen consequences. For, not only did this action signal the beginning of the end of the first Carlist war, but it also marked the beginning of a new era for the Spanish church.

iii

When Mendizábal began the *desamortización* of church lands, he was simply carrying out a tenet of the Liberal creed—land reform. The most aggravating fact about church land was not so much the amount—the Spanish historian Rafael Altamira has estimated that this land had an annual rental income of over one billion *reales* (approximately seventy million 1930 dollars)[3]—but the fact that this land never changed hands. It was held in mortmain. This meant that the lands could not be sold or transferred to an outside party and that they had to be passed on intact to the next generation; furthermore, the church, being a continuous institution, was not affected by inheritance taxes or the division of its landed wealth. The Liberals could see no possibility of economic reform until this land became a productive element (in their terms) of the national economy. In addition, there was in 1835 an extraordinarily large national debt. The government had been in debt ever since the war against Napoleon, and the costs of the Carlist war had added an extra burden.

3. *Historia de España y de la civilización española* (Barcelona, 1911), IV, 236-37. The conversion from *reales* to dollars is in Charles E. Chapman, *A History of Spain* (New York, 1938), p. 454, which coincides with the conversion rates given in other reputable sources.

If the lands were expropriated and sold, the national debt could be considerably reduced.

The Liberals of 1835 did not originate the idea of a *desamortización*—Charles III had expropriated church property and the Liberal governments of 1820-23 had also joined in the confiscation of the church's landed wealth. However, in 1835, the *desamortización* was begun on a full scale.

From 1835 to 1844 most of the church lands were expropriated and disposed of by public auction. The Liberals' plan was to free the land by creating a rural middle class; the proceeds from the sale would defray the governmental debt, and the new class would join the Liberal party and thereby give it much-needed strength. The plan failed miserably. So much land flooded the market that values were depreciated and much of the land was sold for ridiculously low prices. For example, the lands and buildings of the University of Alcalá were sold for fifteen hundred *pesetas* ($360).[4] More important, a rural middle class was not created, for the wealthier Liberals and the large landowners could afford to outbid everyone else; the land was simply transferred to them and it remained concentrated in a few hands.

The *desamortización* created more problems than it solved. It did bring an end to the Carlist war, but in the process laid the foundation for future struggles—not between Liberals and Carlists, but between proletariat and oligarchy. Antonio Ramos-Oliviera, that caustically Marxist historian of modern Spain, quite accurately points out the effects of the *desamortización*.[5] The landlords, tending towards Carlism or actively supporting it,

4. Antonio Ballesteros y Beretta, *Historia de España y su influencia en la historia universal* (Barcelona, 1934-41), VIII, 646.

5. *Politics, Economics and Men of Modern Spain, 1808-1946* (London, 1946), pp. 55-61.

joined in the purchase of the lands; to protect their invest-
ment they now had to support the Liberals, for a Carlist
victory would mean the return of the lands to the church.
They withdrew from the pretender's cause. Most of the
wealthier Liberals, on the other hand, became conservative with the acquisition of newly-acquired wealth, and
they joined the landlords in urging an end to the war,
which was, in fact, effected by the Peace of Vergara of
1839.

Out of this fusion of the main supporters of liberalism
and Carlism a new landed oligarchy was born. Liberalism and Carlism as ideologies did not die out; in fact,
both were purified, although both were left much weaker.
The remaining Carlists took up the cause of regional
separatism, seeking in these movements a source of
strength, and by devious means, attempted to work their
way into the government from within—by becoming confessors and advisors to monarchs. The discarded mantle
of Liberal reform was taken over by the *petit* bourgeoisie
and the intelligentsia, the new democratic liberals. This
reform group accepted most of the original tenets of liberalism—including anticlericalism—but they departed from
classical economic thought to favor the amelioration of
working-class conditions through governmental regulation. All of this did not come about overnight, but it was
a trend in the nineteenth century which reached fruition
in the twentieth. Thus, by the middle of the nineteenth
century four main groups occupied the political stage.
In the center there were the Liberals and Conservatives—
indistinguishable except for the Liberals' anticlericalism—
and on the fringes, right and left respectively, there were
the Carlists and the democratic liberals.

At the same time, the class struggle of modern Spain
came into being, for the *desamortización* was not limited

to church lands. The Liberals also put up for sale the common lands of the municipalities, the public-owned communal lands. These rural folk, dispossessed of their property, formed a new class—the proletariat. Henceforth, the social struggle in Spain was to be one of proletariat versus oligarchy.

The effect of the *desamortización* on the church was of major consequence; it determined, more than anything else, the socio-political role of that institution in modern Spanish history. The loss of its lands meant the loss of its revenues, for rents were the chief source of church income. As a result, most of the clergy were left without financial support. The Liberals tried to solve this problem by imposing a tax upon the people for the support of the clergy, but this proved unsuccessful. When the Conservatives came to power in 1844, they put an end to the *desamortización* and decided that the state should undertake responsibility for the support of the clergy. They legislated that each cleric should get a fixed annuity "sufficient to allow a modest life, taking into account person and place."[6] The main consequence of the establishment of state-paid clerical salaries was that the clergy became more dependent on the state, and at the same time, they became an endless source of irritation to the state. In other words, the clergy became a new bureaucratic group, something of which Spain has always had a surplus.

But state-paid salaries were not enough to support the church; the clergy felt economically insecure. They now felt obliged to curry favor with the new oligarchy—the very group that has dispossessed them—in order to survive and prosper again. This had far-reaching consequences, for it implied taking a partisan position in the social strug-

6. Juan Soto de Gongoiti, *Relaciones de la iglesia católica y el estado español* (Madrid, 1940), p. 80, citing the document.

gle, which was becoming the most important factor in Spanish life. The clergy's support of the wealthy classes meant that they now had to turn their backs to the masses. Thus, a deep chasm was formed between the new oligarchy and the church, on the one hand, and the proletariat on the other. It is from the *desamortización*, then, that the alienation of the masses from the church dates.

iv

After the end of the Carlist war in 1839, Spanish political life took on a calmer tone. Although opposing factions sought power there was no longer open warfare in the nation. Spain had its problems but none seemed important enough to fight over. In 1844 the Conservative party assumed control of the government, and it was determined to consolidate internal peace. One outstanding problem faced the Conservatives—the *desamortización;* they wanted a settlement with the church which would allow them to keep their new property and which would at the same time return religious peace to Spain.

The Conservatives had no hope of a settlement as long as Pope Gregory XVI occupied the pontifical throne. The despoliation of church lands, the anticlerical violence, and the various laws regulating the religious orders had so worsened relations with Rome that the Pope had refused to recognize any Spanish government. The pontiff had gone so far as to condemn Liberal policy in Spain with a papal allocution in 1842. He had consistently refused to allow the consecration of government-appointed bishops to fill vacant ecclesiastical sees, and as a result, by 1845, over one half of Spain's sees were vacant. It was with a sigh of relief then that the government welcomed Gregory's successor in 1846.

Pope Pius IX came to the pontificate free of rancor towards Spain. Indeed, he was favorably disposed towards the Spanish government, particularly after eight thousand Spanish troops helped restore him to the Quirinal after the 1848 revolutions in the Papal States. Accordingly, when the Spanish prime minister, Luis González Bravo, made overtures for an accord with the papal nuncio, Monsignor Giovanni Brunelli, the two parties drafted an agreement that both Pius and Queen Isabella II signed in 1851. This was the concordat of 1851; it remained in force except for brief intervals until 1931.[7]

The concordat was generally favorable to the church, but at the same time it gave the Conservatives what they wanted—the church's acceptance of the *desamortización* as a *fait accompli*. Furthermore the church agreed to sanction the sale of church lands which the state still held, providing the profits were invested in state bonds (to be applied to the national debt) and distributed among the clergy. In return the church's right to acquire any kind of property in the future was recognized.

The concordat reaffirmed the official recognition of Catholicism as "the only religion of the Spanish nation." The church was granted, in effect, the right to control education in the state schools. The clergy's annual stipends, to be paid by the state, were established; these ranged from 160,000 *reales* ($9,600) for the Archbishop of Toledo to 2,200 *reales* ($132) for rural priests. The state also agreed to help maintain church buildings with annuities ranging from 170,000 *reales* ($10,200) to 1,000 *reales* ($60). To defray these expenses, the government

7. For the text and a commentary on the concordat see Jerónimo Becker, *Relaciones diplomáticas entre España y la Santa Sede durante el siglo XIX* (Madrid, 1908), pp. 464-70.

was given the funds of the Santa Cruzada (a church tax for papal privileges), the landed estates of the military orders, and the product of the land that the clergy still owned.

The state gained an important political concession—although one fully in accord with established practice in Spain—the right to nominate ecclesiastical appointees. As the government only nominated those whose loyalty to its principles was unquestioned, it naturally resulted that those in the upper clergy were usually partisans of the old regime in any revolutionary situation. This fact helps to explain the church's hostility to reformist and revolutionary governments.

The concordat was broken in 1855 when the Liberals returned to power and decreed the *desamortización* of the remaining church lands. In 1859 the Conservatives took over the government and signed the Ley del Convenio with the Holy See, a document that reaffirmed the concordat of 1851 but recognized the expropriations of 1855-59. Again, in 1869 the concordat was violated following General Prim's coup and remained so throughout the years of the reign of Amadeo of Savoy and the First Spanish Republic. After the restoration of Alfonso XII in 1874, the constitution of 1876 recognized the concordat with no changes other than allowing a modicum of religious toleration.[8] It then remained in force for just over half a century until the revolution of 1931.

8. See *ibid.*, pp. 471-78, for Cánovas' interpretation of Article 11 of the 1876 document. It is interesting to note that both the Conservative constitution of 1845 and the Liberal document of 1855 declared Catholicism to be the state religion. The latter constitution did allow freedom for nonconformists, as long as they did not "manifest acts contrary to religion." In 1869, with the fall of Isabella II, a new constitution decreed religious freedom for all foreigners resident in Spain and for those Spaniards who formally renounced Catholicism. The 1876 constitution allowed toleration of non-Catholics as long as they made no external display of their religion.

This history of the concordat of 1851 explains its weaknesses. It was in essence an attempt to perpetuate the *status quo* of one fortuitous moment in Spanish history. It wedded both church and state, in their relations with each other, to an outmoded document. Instead of settling relations, it became a prime source of irritation, so much so that by 1930 almost all Spaniards agreed that the concordat needed revision.

By the middle of the nineteenth century, the struggle between church and state had brought little but sorrow to both. The church and the Liberals had both lost their impetus and had become tied to reactionary principles. Neither could offer Spain the guidance needed to cope with its immense problems. On the other hand, the new reformist parties had inherited the legacy of anticlericalism, and thus it came about that the church opposed political, economic, and social reform because, in each case, reform was usually accompanied by anticlericalism.

Furthermore, the struggles of the first half of the nineteenth century had been so intense that there developed a national obsession concerning relations between church and state. This attitude was a preoccupation with religio-political problems, so much so that each time a new government came into existence, it first had to settle relations with the church. So dear did this approach become, that long after the church ceased to present a problem to the state, reformist or otherwise, relations with the church were the primary issue upon which governments rose or fell. This national attitude was nothing less than fatal, for greater problems faced the nation, particularly after 1876, problems which no government could afford to temporize with.

CHAPTER 4

6H5o

THE NATIONAL
AND
RELIGIOUS DISCORD

During the thirty years that followed the Peace of
Vergara, Liberals, Conservatives, and generals alternated
in political control of Spain. While there was little open
strife in the country, a government constantly prey to
coups d'état and open to the influence of a scandalous and
politically incompetent queen could not provide a foundation of stability, especially in view of the growing class
strife that resulted from the *desamortización* of the
church and communal lands. By 1869 the nation, like a
rudderless ship, drifted through the seas of political fortune. Queen Isabella II openly tended towards Carlism,
and in the hands of unscrupulous confessors she became
more absolutist and fanatic. In 1869 the military arose
again—as they had done so often before—but this time
Isabella was exiled, and General Juan Prim became the
head of state.

This military coup, supported by civilians, indicated

the weakness of the moderate reform movement. For, with the queen gone, the Spanish state floundered for two years while Spanish statesmen searched Europe for a monarch to take Isabella's place. They finally obtained the services of Amadeo of Savoy, who ruled as a strict constitutional monarch for a year until, asked by his prime minister to violate the constitution, he abdicated and left the country. The Cortes, having no other recourse, proclaimed the First Spanish Republic.

Spain's first republican experiment was chaos compounded on confusion. In the first place, the Cortes was overwhelmingly monarchist in sentiment; then, there was confusion over the form of government—federalist or centralist—within the republic itself. While these issues were being debated in the Cortes, some of the Spanish cities proclaimed their independence with a type of cantonal government and went to war with the federal government. The Carlists took advantage of the confusion to start an insurrection in northern Spain. It is a wonder that the First Republic survived for the full year it did. In 1874 the army proclaimed a restoration of the Spanish Bourbons in the person of Isabella's son, Alfonso XII.

With the restoration of 1874, Spaniards, for the first time in almost three-quarters of a century, could look forward to the enjoyment of political peace. Seemingly, everyone was tired of political struggles that cost so dearly and that brought nothing but a change of regime. Unfortunately, the government of the restoration provided peace, but little else. Profoundly disturbing problems grew and rankled within the nation and caused discord in Spain's social and intellectual fabric. This inner turmoil affected politico-ecclesiastical relations as well as the internal history of both the state and the church.

i

One of the problems vexing both church and state was the question of the status of the religious orders. Liberal Spaniards had always felt that there were too many regular clerics in Spain; seventeenth- and eighteenth-century reformers often referred to the regulars as drones upon the economic life of the nation, calling them an unproductive element. The problem, however, lay much deeper than this untrue simplification. The root of the controversy was in the relative independence of the regular clergy, for neither the state nor the secular episcopate had effective control over them.

The secular clergy disliked the regulars for a number of reasons. The bishops had little control over them, as the regulars were responsible to their superior who was in turn responsible to Rome. The lower seculars disliked them because the regulars were better educated and because their vow of poverty freed them from financial worry. Furthermore, because the regulars were better educated, the wealthy tended to patronize the regular's churches, causing the secular pastor both financial and psychological grief.

The state had no control over the regulars for it did not control their appointments; they were an ultramontane influence as far as the state was concerned. This influence was especially disturbing because the regulars controlled most of the secondary schools in the country. On the other hand, the state found it easy to legislate against the regulars, because of their disciplined organization.

Of all the religious orders, the Jesuits were the most numerous, best organized, most militant, and wealthiest of all. They ran the finest secondary schools in Spain. However, their superb organization made them the easiest to legislate against, and whenever the anticlerical state moved against the church it usually expelled or dissolved the Jesuits first, before taking other actions to decrease the church's power.

All of these factors led to the peculiar position of the religious orders as defined by the concordat of 1851. In its most controversial provision, the concordat read: "So that there be, in the Peninsula, a sufficient number of priests to assist the sick and dying, to help the prelates in their preaching duties . . . to help the parish priests . . . and to do other works of charity and utility, the government of her Majesty . . . will take the necessary arrangements to establish wherever necessary . . . houses of the religious congregations of St. Vincent de Paul, St. Philip Neri, and another order from those approved by the Holy See . . ."[1]

The ambiguity of this article lent itself to controversial interpretations. The anticlericals understood it to mean that only three orders were to be allowed in all of Spain. The clergy had varying interpretations: some maintained that a different third order could be established in each diocese; others that all orders were free to come and go until Rome named the third (which Rome never did); and still others argued that because the government agreed to establish and support three orders, all others which could survive without governmental assistance were free to do so. All of these interpretations were rationalizations of the fact that the religious orders were a problem in Spanish religious life.

After the restoration of 1874 the religious orders multiplied rapidly. In 1877, the Cortes passed a Law of Associations (aimed at controlling labor unions) that required all organizations to register with the government. As the

1. Becker, *Relaciones diplomáticas,* p. 467.

law excluded those religious orders named in the concordat, no order felt obliged to comply. In 1901, a mildly
anticlerical government commanded all orders to register
under this law. The Holy See protested, and the government retracted the decree. Then, the controversy was
renewed by two external events—the 1905 separation of
church and state in France, and the anticlerical persecu-
tions of the nascent Portuguese Revolution in 1910. Many
of the French and Portuguese regulars sought refuge in
Spain. The government now felt that it had cause for
action, for the idea of Gallican clerics teaching in Spanish
schools was repugnant to many Spaniards. The prime
minister, José Canalejas, introduced the Ley del Can-
dado, or Padlock Law, in the Cortes. This law forbade
the establishment of new orders or *conventos* with less
than two-thirds of the members being Spanish citizens.
The Holy See protested, but the law was passed. However, the king was brought around to support the church's
position and the law was allowed to lapse after a two-year
period. Thus, all governmental attempts to control the
religious orders failed, and the regulars continued to
increase.

ii

If the problem of the religious orders—whether real or
imaginary—troubled both the Spanish government and
the secular episcopate, the problem of educational
reform was more disturbing and had profounder consequences. The conflict over educational reform revolved
around two concepts of education—religious and secular.
It was a conflict similar to that in many European countries, except that in Spain the opposing forces wanted
their aims carried to extremes. The church had always
defended its control of education, for it claimed to be the

guardian of the faithful in all matters; it wanted all teaching to be religion-oriented. On the other hand, the democratic liberals wanted a secular school system; they defined secular as laic; and they wanted the church excluded from the intellectual life of the nation. This division resulted in a basic conflict in Spanish intellectual life. Those who defended the church came to be known as the Apologistas, while the secular reformers took up the philosophy of the German Karl Friedrich Krause (1781-1832) and became known as the Krausistas.

The Catholic Apologistas were a mediocre flowering of the old Catholic intellectual tradition. Their main driving force was a fear of new ideas. In many respects forced to this position by the Liberal-Carlist struggles, they concerned themselves with a morbid fear of Protestantism (which was virtually nonexistent in Spain) and continually rephrased the theme that only traditionalism could give Spain the political and religious unity it needed. Theirs was a purely negative approach to Spain's problems, and it was a great contrast to Catholic thought of the sixteenth century. The intellectual decline of the church was nowhere more evident than in a comparison of Suárez and Vittoria with Juan Donoso Cortés or even Jaime Balmes. Furthermore, the Apologistas' constant concern with the dangers of Protestantism and liberalism helps to account for the scant attention they gave to the more pressing problems of the nation—those of responsible education and an intelligent approach to the social problem. It was not until the decades immediately preceding the Second Republic that some Catholic thinkers awakened to these more immediate concerns.

Many of the secular intellectuals subscribed to a philosophy that had found fertile ground only in Spain—Krausism. This school of thought, which was more a cultural approach than a systematic ideology, hoped to solve Spain's problems through rationalistic education and a questioning attitude.[2] They held that man's nature could be perfected by humanistic education and social justice. The Krausistas were deeply concerned with the social problem, but because they were not in a position of influence, they were unable to provide a solution to the workingman's immediate needs.

The founder of Spanish Krausism was Julián Sánz del Río, an educator who had studied in Germany. However, it was Francisco Giner de los Ríos who came to personify the intellectual movement. After he was forced out of his position at the University of Madrid in 1874, Giner de los Ríos founded a private school, the Institución Libre de Enseñanza, which had great success. He also helped establish the Junta para Amplificación de Estudios, an organization to help students study abroad. Despite these advances, however, the Krausistas represented only a minority of the Spanish intellectuals. Their immediate hindrance was official disapproval and lack of money, for the church was given control of public education by the terms of the concordat of 1851 and had funds to foment its educational aims.

Therefore, the church controlled public education, and it taught with a definite Carlist bent. In 1836, the state took the universities out of the hands of the church, and they remained so thereafter, but the church's influence was still felt. In the primary and secondary schools, the church's power was paramount; the state simply preempted secondary education to the church and the religious orders. Although primary education was still

2. See Abbé Pierre Jobit, *Les Éducateurs de l'Espagne moderne* (Paris, 1936), and Juan López Morillas, *El Krausismo español: Perfil de una aventura intelectual* (México, 1956).

nominally under the control of the state, there was little difference between the public schools and the church schools. In either one, religion was taught almost to the exclusion of everything else. Gerald Brenan notes that "the difference between a convent school and a state school was not one of religion but of politics. To put it bluntly the children in convent schools were taught that if they associated with Liberals, they went to hell."[3]

Two factors help to explain the decline in education. First, the state was not anxious to support a public school system controlled by the church, and it gradually reduced the educational budget. Second, the 1869 suppression of the faculties of theology in the universities was continued in force, and this resulted in the restriction of priestly training to the seminaries where the young clergy had no contact with lay students or teachers. As José Castillejo, a disinterested observer commented: "A new priest would learn political novelties only by listening to their dogmatic detractors."[4] Consequently, the clergy remained ignorant and intolerant, and their students followed the same pattern. Furthermore, those clerics who were interested in improving themselves became more dependent on the wealthy for money to purchase books and to maintain their seminaries.

The result of the educational decline was that by 1910 half of the population was still illiterate. By 1931, even in the larger cities, less than half of the children attended school. The liberal intelligentsia had come to look upon

3. *Spanish Labyrinth*, p. 51. The standard catechisms used in both schools, even today, have condemnations of liberalism. These are Santiago José García Mazo, *El catecismo de la doctrina cristiana* (36th ed.; Valladolid, 1924), and Jerónimo Martínez de Ripalda, *El catecismo de la doctrina cristiana* (40th ed.; Madrid, 1934).

4. *War of Ideas in Spain: Philosophy, Politics, and Education* (London, 1937), p. 87.

the church as the enemy of modern culture, and the church had settled into what Salvador de Madariaga calls its role of "strife and division."[5] This view of the church's disruption of national life was reflected in a new intellectual movement during the twentieth century, that approach originated by the "Generation of '98." These important thinkers, including Miguel de Unamuno, José Ortega y Gasset, Joaquín Costa, Ángel Ganivet, Pío Baroja, "Azorín," and later Gregorio Marañón and Ramón Pérez de Ayala, were seriously disturbed by the loss of the last remnants of Spain's colonial power and international prestige in the Spanish-American War of 1898. They felt that Spain should re-examine her past and some wanted Spaniards to look for new methods and ways of development. Their questioning attitude forced Spaniards to think more realistically and led many people to wonder if Catholicism was indeed a necessary element of Spanish life.

iii

By the latter part of the nineteenth century both the problems of the religious orders and of educational reform were eclipsed in intensity by the social question, Spain's most important single problem. Bred by the agrarian problem, it in turn intensified the religious problem; these three have been inseparable in recent Spanish history. If the social problem had not aggravated the politico-ecclesiastical struggle, the latter would have been confined to the intellectual and political arenas, as in Germany and France. As it was, the Spanish conflict led to civil war.

The basic problem in Spanish economic life is agrarian. Climate and geography have helped create this problem:

5. *Spain: A Modern History* (New York, 1958), p. 169.

where the soil is rich, there is little rainfall, while the unproductive areas receive an abundance of moisture. In this manner, northern Spain, wet, with poor soil, developed into an area of small landholdings. As this area had been comparatively free of the Moslem influence, it evolved much like the rest of western Europe. Southern and central Spain are dry areas, and it was here that the great latifundia existed.

Until the nineteenth century Spain's economic problems were pastoral, not agrarian. The peasants had communal lands that they sometimes tilled, but generally the pastoral elements controlled the land. Successive ministries of the eighteenth century tried to remedy this pastoral problem by disentailing the estates of the lesser nobility. When the Liberals came to power, they broke the entailed pastoral hold on Spain with the *desamortización*. The church and communal lands were turned over to agricultural production, and a new oligarchy took control of the land.

The new landed oligarchy did not live on their estates. Thus, to the harsh climatic conditions of the south which permitted only a minimal working of the land, there were added the abuses of absentee landlordism. Concomitantly, the problems of an increasing population helped reduce the agrarian proletariat of these areas to a semisubsistant living standard. In the north, meanwhile, the small landholders had credit problems and were forced to go to the same landed oligarchy for their needs. These problems were still pressing when the industrial revolution came to Spain.

The bourgeois oligarchy introduced industrialism, although on a smaller scale than in any other western European nation. Industrialism produced the same problems it had elsewhere in Europe, with sweatshop conditions and long working hours. But the Spanish urban proletariat was smaller, in proportion, than its counterpart in France, Germany, and England. Furthermore, industrial violence became unavoidable because there was no political framework within which the workers could channel their demands. Industrial problems aggravated existing tensions and Spain, like prerevolutionary Russia, had to face the problems of the machine age along with an unsolved agrarian problem. Much of the industrial capital was supplied by foreign investors who were unaware of the nation's problems, and a miserable industrial proletariat was created alongside the agrarian laborers.

A rigid social stratification was formed. There was the landed and industrial oligarchy, and there was the proletariat. A deep chasm separated the two. Unlike the other western countries, Spain had no firm middle class to serve as a buffer between rich and poor and to serve as a step in the ladder of social mobility. There was no movement from the lower to the upper classes. If the agrarian worker were dissatisfied, his only choice, if he could afford it, was to move to the city and become an industrial worker. He would receive a small increase in wages, but the problems of urban living would offset it. This was the social problem: a small group receiving the large majority of the national income while the great masses lived in squalor and semistarvation. There came to be a justifiable spirit of bitter class hatred of the poor for the rich. Government policy exacerbated these conditions, since it was in the hands of an oligarchy accustomed to using all forms of political corruption to further its aims. The proletariat's response to the social problem was socialism and anarchism.

The utopian working class movements that had become widespread throughout Europe by the latter half of the nineteenth century did not bypass Spain. The Socialist party, based on Marxian principles, was founded in Spain in 1879, and developed strength chiefly through the efforts of Pablo Iglesias. The Socialists attracted the urban proletariat of all the Spanish cities except Barcelona and developed into the largest working-class party. Iglesias' revision of Marxism into a nonviolent movement that hoped to further its aims through legitimate political action accounted for much of the strength of the party. In 1888, the Socialists founded the Unión General de Trabajadores (UGT), which came to be the most important and influential of all the Spanish trade unions. The Socialist party was fairly authoritarian, but on the whole it represented a mild type of socialism.

International anarchism, founded by Michael Bakunin (1814-86), was introduced in Spain by the founder's disciple, Giusèppe Fanelli, in 1868. It quickly spread among the industrial workers of Barcelona and the agrarian laborers of Andalusia.[6] The anarchists' approach to the social problem was almost evangelical: they desired a return to simplicity, especially in religious matters, an egalitarian distribution of private property among individuals (as opposed to Socialist collectivism), and above all, they wanted local autonomy. The anarchists shunned all political activity until they united with the revolutionary syndicalist movement which had developed among the working classes of Barcelona. Revolutionary syndicalism, based on the Sorelian theory of the general strike, was admirably suited to Spanish anarchism because both movements emphasized a violent overthrow of the existing political and social structure. In 1910, these new

6. See Gabriel Jackson, "The Origins of Spanish Anarchism," *Southwestern Social Science Quarterly*, XXXVI (September, 1955), pp. 135-47; and the classic on Andalusian anarchism, J. Díaz del Moral, *Historia de las agitaciones campesinas andaluzas* (Córdoba, Madrid, 1929).

anarcho-syndicalists organized a trade union, the Confederación Nacional del Trabajo (CNT), and formed a political party based on the technique of violence.

The nature of the church's response to the social problem must be viewed against this background of utopian working-class movements and the whole struggle between liberalism and traditionalism. Partly because of the Socialists' economic determinism and the anarchists' violent methods, but mainly because anticlericalism was a major tenet of all reformist groups, the church could not support any of them. Even more important, socialism and anarchism were antireligious movements. For the church, the essential element of its existence was the maintenance of peace and order; only under these conditions did the clergy feel that they could carry out their mission. The oligarchy's promise of peace and order, even if enforced by a corrupt hand, was preferable to the anticlerical violence of the mob.

Because of the great gulf that separated rich and poor, the church could not stay neutral and it was called upon to take sides. On the one side there were the poor, the secular working-class movements to compete against, poverty, and the antagonism of the wealthy and the government. On the other side there were the wealthy, sufficient funds for the church to foment its aims, a favored position with the government, and what the clergy felt was a good standpoint from which to fight secular socialism and godless anarchism. The most powerful elements in the church chose the latter position, and the church lost the working classes.

This is not to say that the clergy did not speak out against social misery; many influential voices declaimed against the actions of the wealthy classes—pastorals were written, studies of Pope Leo XIII's social encyclicals anpeared, and sermons were preached.[7] But, the clergy's alliance with the oligarchy outweighed any steps it took to mitigate social evils. The clergy failed to realize that the solution of the social problem should have been found in governmental legislation and the realities of a strong trade union movement, not the inward persuasion of pastoral letters and papal encyclicals.

The church did not act as a unit. Indeed, no problem shows the division within it more concretely. Generally, the episcopate opposed social and political action by reformist groups. After years of liberal experiments and civil wars, the hierarchy found itself in an influential position in Spanish political life and was loath to upset the power balance. Implicit in this position was a refusal to recognize a workable solution to the social problem. The workers' response of anticlerical violence served only to confirm the episcopate in its attitude.

This view was not so prevalent among the lower clergy since these priests dealt directly with the lower classes, and in most cases were recruited from them.[8] However, because of their low salaries they were more dependent upon the wealthy than were the bishops. Poorly educated and faced with the strong penetration of socialism and anarcho-syndicalism among their parishioners, the enormity of their problem caused the lower clergy to lose all

7. For example, see Victoriano Guisasola y Menéndez, Archbishop of Valencia, *La acción social del clero* (Valencia, 1910), a pastoral calling for more active social interests from the clergy; later, as Cardinal-Archbishop of Toledo, *Justicia y caridad en la organización cristiana del trabajo* (Madrid, 1916), calling for recognition of workingmen's rights and condemning proprietors for the low wages they paid. See also, Juan Maura y Gelabert, Bishop of Orihuela, *La cuestión social* (Madrid, 1902), for a series of pastorals completely in line with Pope Leo XIII's *Rerum novarum*.

8. Gabriel Palau, S. J., ed., *Diario íntimo de un cura español (1919-1931)* (Barcelona, 1932), the diary of an anonymous urban pastor, is one of the most illuminating works on the problems of the lower clergy.

hope. They lapsed into pious undertakings and were unable to provide any leadership toward a solution of the problem.

The religious orders occupied an ambiguous position. While many had no direct contact with the people, others, such as the Dominicans, were active in social labors. The Jesuits' position illustrated the division that rent the church as a whole: they were the most active in cultivating the upper classes through their school system; they antagonized the wealthy by their commercial enterprises and favored economic position with the government; finally, some of the Jesuits published and demonstrated one of the soundest approaches to the social problem, the formation of a sound trade union movement.

Among Catholics, it was a group of laymen who worked the hardest to resolve the problem. Motivated by the social teachings of Pope Leo XIII, they were the forerunners of the Christian democratic movement in Spain. These thinkers and workers formed and supported Catholic trade unions, consumer cooperatives, agrarian credit unions, and agrarian syndicates. Their greatest obstacle was the opposition of the oligarchy, who felt that any deviation from unbridled individualism was suspect and heretical. They were opposed even within the church; one of their leaders described their difficulties: "Our adversaries are not only the Socialists, Anarchists, and Liberal politicians: they are also the Catholic *beati possidenti* who denounce us as revolutionaries to the bishops."[9]

The Catholic trade union movement was successful only in the Basque provinces, where the social problem was the least aggravated and where the workers were able to support unions. In the other areas, the church's

9. Severino Aznar y Embid in 1908, cited in Angel Marvaud, *La Question sociale en Espagne* (Paris, 1910), p. 208.

view was that employers and employees should be organized in the same union. This approach led to control by the employers, and the Catholic unions thereby became ineffective in voicing working class demands. Thus, the workers quite naturally joined the Socialist unions and bitterly denounced the Catholic unions as being controlled by the employers.

The first Catholic trade unions, the Centros Católicos de Obreros, were organized in 1861 by Father Antonio Vicent, S.J. They were successful until they ran out of money. In the south, the Centros died out under the pressure of the underground activities of the Anarchists. Socialism and anarchism had made great inroads by the time the Centros were revived, and they were no longer large enough to be effective. At this juncture, the bishops suggested that the employers "patronize" the Catholic unions by providing them with funds. This, of course, ended their usefulness in the south. In northern Spain, where the social problem was less acute, the Centros flourished for a time, but soon they also ran out of funds; employers were asked to aid them, and the workers lost interest.

After the Centros died out, the church suggested that Acción Católica organize the workers. Because of its organizational structure, Acción Católica was not suited to the demands of a working class movement and it proved unsuccessful against the effectiveness of the secular unions.

Generally, Catholic unions contrasted unfavorably with the superior organization of the Socialist unions, which in many industries had a closed-shop monopoly. The Socialists denounced the Catholic unions for splitting the workingman's front and looked upon them as tools in the employers' hands.

Only in Catalonia and Vizcaya was the Catholic trade

union movement successful. Here, the Federación Nacional de Sindicatos Católicos Libres was founded by Dominican priests in 1912. The Federación became a unit of the Christian Trade Union International and it developed into a true working-class movement with ample funds. It used all of the traditional weapons of union warfare, and often joined with the Socialist unions to achieve common objectives. By 1928, the Federación numbered forty thousand members; it was the only Catholic union that lost no strength during the years of the Second Republic.

The church was more successful in the agrarian field, where it concerned itself with providing credit organizations. Since Spanish banks were notoriously loath to extend credit, the church had a good opportunity to help the small farmer. Under its patronage, the Banco Popular de León XIII was organized. This bank lent money at fair interest rates (4 to 7 per cent) to small farmers and artisans. At the same time, the Sindicatos Católicos de Agrícolas developed, with equally low credit rates. The big credit organization was the Confederación Nacional Católico Agraria, founded in 1912.[10] However, all of these organizations soon came under the control of the grain-producing oligarchy and lent their money for a price besides interest—that of votes for Catholic-conservative candidates. This political use of church-controlled credit helps to account for conservative-clerical strength in the rural areas.

Therefore, while the church's organization of the working class generally met with failure, it was not because the church lacked ambition. Its lack of success was prin-

10. By 1926, this organization had buildings valued at 20 million pesetas, deposits of 250 million, and loans totalling 200 million. Ramos-Oliviera, *Politics, Economics and Men*, pp. 252-53.

cipally the result of the d*esamortización*. The church had to court the wealthy to regain its economic power, and it had to support them to see peace and order maintained. This meant it had to approve, tacitly or otherwise, the oppression of the lower classes. And, to the lower classes, what sealed the argument against the church and its stand on the social question was that same economic power that the church so eagerly sought.

iv

The reputed wealth of the Spanish church has been a constant source of ammunition for anticlericals and of embarrassment for Catholics. As noted, there are historical reasons for the church's desire for economic power. But, the form of wealth it sought after the *desamortización* made an important difference. Having been dispossessed of its landed wealth numerous times by Liberal regimes, the church decided to place its new wealth in industrial and commercial investments that could easily be liquidated should persecution come again. The years of restoration peace enabled it to carry out this policy, which had two important results. The investments, being "secret," were exaggerated and gave rise to the belief that the church possessed enormous wealth. Of more consequence, the church lost contact with the working classes, something that could not have happened had it possessed landed wealth. As Franz Borkenau comments, "Never would the masses have been driven away from a church fixed on the land; they were easily led to abandon a church which was the richest shareholder in the community."[11]

Aside from investments, the sources of secular clerical

11. *The Spanish Cockpit: An Eyewitness Account of the Political and Social Conflicts of the Spanish Civil War* (London, 1937), p. 9.

wealth were the stipends fixed by the concordat, the Cruzada, fees from various pious organizations, fees in some parishes for the performance of the sacraments, and what landed wealth remained to the clergy. The value of the latter was estimated to be 129,000,000 *pesetas* ($24,510,000) in 1930.[12] In the same year, the state paid out 66,000,000 *pesetas* ($12,540,000) in clerical salaries; this sum was distributed among 32,000 priests. It is impossible to determine the amount the secular clergy had invested. The greatest complaint about this wealth was its uneven distribution, for the income of some of the bishops was all out of proportion to that of the lower clergy, who were often as poor as their parishioners. Jaime Torrubiano Ripoll, an admitted anticlerical, estimated that the Bishop of Madrid-Alcalá had an annual income of 284,000 *pesetas* ($54,150).[13]

While this situation led to increasing friction within clerical ranks, it was the wealth of the religious orders, particularly the Jesuits, which excited the most comment. Because they invested in commercial and mercantile activities, they aroused the ire of the democratic liberals and the oligarchy alike. Wise to the ways of government expropriation, they registered many of their investments in the names of laymen or "straw men." The legendary estimate of their property was one-third of the capital wealth of Spain.[14] Subsequent confiscations of Jesuit

12. Ramos-Oliviera, *Politics, Economics and Men*, pp. 435-37, who admits his figures to be only an approximation. The figures were compiled by the Republican Ministry of Justice in 1931.

13. *Beatería y religión: Meditaciones de un canonista* (Madrid, 1930), pp. 33-34. The complaint of the uneven distribution of church wealth is commented on in L. Aizpún, "Hemos Fracasado," *Revista Eclesiástica*, 56 (April, 1936), 361-72 (this article was originally published in 1928).

14. As far as I have been able to determine, the original source of this frequently-quoted statement is attributed to Joaquín Aguilera, in an article in *La Revue* (1912), cited in Angel Marvaud, *L'Espagne au XXe*

property proved these estimates to be greatly exaggerated. However, the British traveler, Rafael Shaw, noted that: "The popular suspicion of Jesuit interference in almost all . . . the big commercial concerns in the peninsula may or may not be justified, but its effect on the attitude of the people toward the religious orders cannot be overrated."[15]

Money is necessary for the administration of dioceses, churches, and schools; few persons can deny that bishops should have sufficient funds to provide for them. In relation to other countries with a similar proportion of clergy to population, the wealth of the church in Spain was not overly large. But in proportion to the working-man's wages, in view of the social problem, and especially in the fact that to get and keep this wealth the clergy was obliged to court the wealthy and neglect the poor, the possession of economic power amounted to an indictment of the episcopate and the religious orders. As a result the working classes saw no reason to practice the faith of a church that they felt had deserted them.

Statistical studies made by the clergy themselves show these results. As early as 1900, the Cardinal-Archbishop of Toledo reported that only 4 per cent of the Madrid populace fulfilled their Easter duty (received the Eucharist at least once a year) and only 5 per cent received the last sacraments.[16] In 1924, the Bishop of Málaga determined that less than one-tenth of the people in his

siecle (Paris, 1913), p. 189, note 1: ". . . on peut évaluer sans exagération à environ le tiers de la richesse nationale les biens, meubles et immeubles, possédés par les congrégations. . . . Les chemins de fer du Nord, la compagnie transatlantique, les orangeries de l'Andalousie, les mines des provinces basques et du Rif, plusieurs des usines de Barcelone, sont sous leurs, emprise avouée on occulte." Brenan, *Spanish Labyrinth*, p. 48, says the Jesuits' working capital was rumoured to be $300 million.

15. *Spain from Within* (London, 1910), p. 93.

16. E. Vargas Zúñiga, S. J., "El problema religioso de España," *Razón y Fe*, 462-63 (July-August, 1935), 302.

diocese attended mass on Sundays.[17] Father Francisco Pieró's famous study of the Church of San Ramón in Vallecas (Madrid), a well-staffed and well-endowed parish, showed that only 7 per cent of the parishioners (including school children) attended mass on Sundays, fewer than one-tenth complied with their Easter duty, and one-fourth of the children born in the parish were not baptized.[18] Pieró reported that in the central rural areas of Spain only 10 per cent of the people practiced their religion faithfully. While almost all these rural folk had their children baptized, were married in, and buried from, the church, they had no other contact with it.

There were other conditions contributing to the apostasy of the working classes. The lack of parochial reorganization, the physical misery of the workers, the shortage of priests, the inroads of socialism, and especially the psychological transformation many workers underwent in moving from the country to the city were all factors. However, the primary cause of this apostasy was the church's desertion of the people. To the workers, religion presented itself as the patrimony of the bourgeoisie, and they formed a simple mental association—church and the wealthy against the poor without religion.

The national and religious discord of the later nineteenth and early twentieth centuries seriously weakened the church. While the church could admit much of the

17. Juan de Iturralde, *El catolicismo y la cruzada de Franco* (Vienne, France, 1955), I, 221.

18. *El problema religioso-social de España* (2nd ed.; Madrid, 1936), pp. 13-14. It is necessary to recall that all of these statistics were based on the percentage of the total population of a parish or area, since Spain was assumed to be wholly Catholic. Thus, Pieró's study of San Ramón parish is based on the total population of the barrio of Vallecas, which was estimated to be 80,000 persons. Pieró's study was made during the years of the republic when anticlerical persecution and the fear many Catholics had of losing their jobs made them hesitant in declaring their religious practices.

responsibility for the problems of the religious orders and educational decline, the secular politicians were primarily responsible for the social problem; the other national problems paled into insignificance in comparison with that festering sore upon the body politic. As a result, class warfare, industrial and agrarian violence, and church burning came to be regular occurrences in Spain. It was little wonder then, that the politicians of the twentieth century failed in most of their tasks. The problems of Spain, by 1930, had become truly enormous.

CHAPTER 5

THE RESTORATION,
THE DICTATORSHIP,
AND THE SPANISH CHURCH

i

Alfonso XII was proclaimed king of Spain in 1874; by this time the nation was profoundly weary of war, fraternal struggles, and of Liberal-Carlist conflicts. The statesmen of the restoration realized this fact, and they therefore were determined to give the nation peace. In itself, this aim was noteworthy; however, their method of attaining peace was not. In the face of internal discord and an exacerbated social problem, the restoration statesmen simply clamped on the lid; they sat on the top of a volcano of tension. As a result of this negative policy, when the revolution finally came, it was much more intense than any upheaval of the nineteenth century.

The chief architect of restoration peace was Antonio Cánovas del Castillo. An historian by profession, he thought that he knew Spain's problems, and he was determined that peace and political stability should precede attempts at social reform; he did not realize that the two should have gone hand in hand and that neither should have been delayed. Cánovas' plan, nonetheless, was to insure stability by creating a pattern of government by alternation between Liberals and Conservatives (the names were labels; both were the oligarchy), and he expelled the army from political life. The cornerstone of his policy was controlled elections—the *cacique* system— whereby the landowners or local political bosses were responsible for turning in "favorable" election results. The inevitable result was, of course, the breakdown of responsible parliamentary government. Cánovas' system was static; because of this, the opposition forces were able to polarize their discontent and channel it into revolutionary activities.

The army, long the arbiter of politics, now fell to plotting against government by civilians. The democratic liberals, resentful of the oligarchy's corrupt rule, wasteful bureaucratic methods, and controlled elections, agitated for a return to constitutional government. The masses, cut off from any sort of legal redress for their social grievances, simply became more revolutionary and joined the utopian working-class organizations. The ultimate result of Cánovas' policy was to bring the army to power in 1923, the democratic liberals to power in 1931, and the masses to power in 1936.

Even Cánovas' aim of political stability was realized for only a few years. By the time that Alfonso XIII came to the throne in 1902 the first violent expression of discontent was in the offing; it occurred in Barcelona in 1909, when the Catalans fought the government.

The Catalan conflict had deep roots. Catalans had always been at odds with the Madrid government because they felt themselves to have been the economic supporters of the nation, while political control had always emanated from Madrid. In times of economic prosperity and efficient government (few, to be sure, in Spanish history), there was little cause for complaint. However, during the tense and troublesome nineteenth century the Catalans began a movement for national self-determination. This movement was helped by a nationalistic renaissance of Catalan literary traditions and by the development of anarcho-syndicalism in Barcelona, for the anarcho-syndicalists were fervent advocates of local and regional autonomy.

In 1909 the Spanish government called out the Catalan reserves to action against the Riffs in the ever-present Moroccan war. The Catalan masses rebelled. Many were inspired by the rumor—perhaps true—that the government's aims were to safeguard Jesuit-owned mines in Morocco. The Catalan democratic liberals joined the fray, for they were resentful of the Madrid government's reactionary and anti-Catalan policies. During the fighting there was an outbreak of anticlericalism and priests were killed and churches were burned in Barcelona; the week of violence was appropriately named the *semana trágica*. The only way the government could put down the Catalans was to call out the troops, and from that moment the army found its role of political arbiter again.

The Catalans were quelled, but the problem was by no means settled. It was subdued momentarily when the economy of the country improved somewhat as Spain played the role of a prosperous neutral during World War I. Immediately after the war however, the inevitable post-war depression was felt. As unemployment rose and wages fell the anarcho-syndicalists and Socialists called a strike in Barcelona. The government, once more, had to call out the troops. By this time the workers' radicalism had frightened the conservative Catalans into supporting the Madrid government's policy. More tension resulted as the conflict took on the nature of a class war. The workers called a general strike in Barcelona in 1919, and they held out for over a year; violence and severe repressions resulted. The army had to take over the situation and the military governor of Catalonia ruled absolutely in that region.

By 1921 it appeared to be only a matter of time until the army would stage a coup and take over the government. The Cortes was, if anything, less efficient than ever. The king was not adverse to a military coup; he had always shown a penchant for the uniform, and he hoped that the army would restore his waning popularity. The event that precipitated the coup was the military disaster at Anual in Morocco in 1921. A parliamentary commission investigated the criminally inefficient planning of the battle, and all evidence seemed to point to Alfonso's complicity. As popular indignation mounted, the king saw that he had only two courses open to him: to give in to the people or to give in to the army. To salvage what personal prestige he could, he chose the latter, and General Miguel Primo de Rivera established a military dictatorship in 1923.

Primo de Rivera was not a politician, but he did conciliate the nation at first. Some very notable reforms were accomplished; the Moroccan War was settled, many public works projects were undertaken, and an honest attempt was made to improve labor relations by setting up arbitration boards. However, because his policy soon degenerated into one of bread and circuses, the dictatorship soon became a strong focus of discontent. By 1930 he had lost all support and the army forced him to resign in January of that year.

With Primo de Rivera's downfall, political affairs became critical. The reformist groups began actively agitating for an immediate solution to the crisis, and few precluded revolutionary means to this end. In view of this revolutionary agitation, the church, along with the army and the oligarchy, was apprehensive. The clergy were aware of the fact that the church could not present a united front against revolution. For, if the body politic of the nation showed an almost unbridgeable division within itself, the church also exhibited a similar discord.

ii

Along with the decline in the Spanish church brought on by the social problem and its attendant evils, there was also a deep political and ideological division within the church. This disunion could be attributed to the revival —or rather the persistence—of Carlism.

Although Carlism lost much of its strength after the *desamortización,* it never died out completely. If anything, its true adherents appeared more devoted to its cause, for the years since 1839 appeared to prove the validity of their contention that liberalism had ruined Spain. And so, from their reactionary, agrarian bastions, the Carlists continued to fight liberal Spain. During the year of chaos surrounding the First Republic, they armed the *requetés* and marched on the towns of northern Spain. After the restoration of 1874, however, they were left deserted by Pope Pius IX's recognition of Alfonso XII, which was a blow to the pretender's cause. They felt their loss even more because the 1876 constitution granted a small degree of religious toleration. On the other hand, they took comfort from some of Pope Pius' other actions, particularly the publication of the *Syllabus of Errors* of 1864.

The *Syllabus* condemned, among other things, separation of church and state and, more important to the Carlists, the idea that "The Roman Pontiff can and ought to reconcile himself to, and agree with Progress, Liberalism, and Modern Civilization." Despite the attempts of Pius' interpreters and of his successor, Leo XIII, to modify and explain these statements, the Carlists found them ideally suited to their political objectives. With this added psychological strength they continued to support the regional autonomy movements in northern Spain, and they formed a new political organization, the Traditionalist party. Then, they proceeded to derogatorily lump together as "liberal Catholics" the moderate Catholics who did not join them. Thus, early in the restoration period there appeared a division in the church.

A bitter polemical war broke out between the two groups despite papal and episcopal efforts at mediation. Then, a third, more reactionary group, the Integrists, was founded by Ramón Nocedal, son of the Traditionalist leader, Cándido Nocedal. The Traditionalists thereby found themselves in the more conciliatory middle position, from which they gained added strength. Pope Leo took an active interest in reconciling the groups, but it was not until Ramón Nocedal died in 1907 that the struggle was ended. However, the breach between the moderate Catholics and the Traditionalists was never healed.

As religious issues came to take on a more civil character, especially after the *semana trágica* in Barcelona, and in view of the rift between groups of Catholics, the fall of the Conservative ministry in 1910 was the occasion of a request from Spanish Catholics to Pope Pius X to clarify the civil duties of Catholics. The Pope responded with a pontifical letter, *Inter Catholicos Hispanae*, in which he stated that Catholics had an obligation to support those candidates "who offer solid guarantees for the good of religion and country." He emphasized that Spaniards should always aim at the re-establishment of religious unity: "It is moreover, the Catholic's obligation to combat those errors reproved by the Holy See, especially those of the *Syllabus of Errors,* and of the dangerous liberties proclaimed by ... Liberalism, whose influence upon the Spanish government is the occasion of such evils."[1]

Pope Pius' view was amplified and interpreted in a letter from the Papal Secretary of State, Rafael Cardinal Merry del Val, to the Archbishop of Toledo, Cardinal Aguirre y García in 1911. Merry del Val warned Spanish Catholics that they had to be certain of the exact meaning of the liberalism condemned by the Pope, and he offered this interpretation: as long as a political party did not tamper with religion or morality, the church could neither condemn nor approve it. Catholics, he noted, were free to organize political parties based on Catholic principles, but they could not criticize other Catholics for not joining them—an obvious aside to the Traditionalists. He also emphasized that no Catholic party could be revolutionary in principle or method.[2]

While Merry del Val's views gave some support to the moderate Catholics, the Traditionalists continued to foster the idea that the Spanish Catholicism of the sixteenth century was not a part of forgotten history but a prologue to the future. They claimed that Spanish Catholicism was consubstantial with the monarchy and that to attack one was to attack the other—a very dangerous position in those waning years of the monarchy. One of the outstanding proponents of this view was Monsignor Zacarías Martínez Núñez, Archbishop of Santiago, whose fiery

1. August 25, 1910, cited in Palau, *Diario íntimo,* pp. 21-22.
2. April 20, 1911, cited in *ibid.,* pp. 22-24, note 1.

nationalistic sermons recalled the glories of both church and monarchy in the sixteenth century.[3] In the face of growing opposition from the democratic liberals and the working-class movements, this idea was an attempt to unite Catholics by using their least common denominator, the monarchy.

By 1930 the division among Catholics had reached major proportions. The church was unable to present a united front to the common danger of anticlericalism and antireligion. The Holy See stepped into this breach with a new organization that claimed to be above the political struggle.

iii

The church's new organization was Catholic Action, the papacy's answer to the spirit of secularism spreading throughout the world. It was an organization of the Catholic laity participating in the work of the church under the direction of the clergy; in this, it represented a positive approach to the church's problems and involved a new concept in allowing the laity this role. As a political influence Catholic Action was strong in those countries which had large Catholic populations.

In those nations where Catholics were struggling against anticlerical parties, how was Catholic Action to maintain itself in its professed "above the partisan level" approach? Its proponents observed that there were two types of politics: "low," which was the action of a particular partisan party working for its own aims, and "high," the art of governing a people in accordance with the common good. The latter was the sphere of Catholic Action; its aim was to avoid identifying the church with

3. Zacarías Martínez Núñez, O.S.A., *Discursos y oraciones sagradas* (2nd ed.; El Escorial, 1929).

one political party and at the same time to leave the church free to influence political life.[4]

Ordinarily, Catholic Action was unconcerned with politics. Only when the church's rights were threatened did it enter the political arena. The fondest hopes of the Catholic Action leaders were to use the organization to safeguard the church's rights before political battles should ensue. From the church's point of view, Catholic Action seemed especially suited to the Spanish church's needs.

Acción Católica (as Catholic Action was known in Spain) was founded in Spain in 1912, but it was disorganized at first because of a typical Spanish tendency to split theological hairs. The movement was not given strong direction until 1921 when the new nuncio, Monsignor Federico Tedeschini, arrived in Madrid and took charge of the organization. Tedeschini applied the organization's aims to social action rather than political, and he asked that well-to-do Catholics show more concern for the poor in the spirit of the teachings of Pope Leo XIII.[5]

During the decade of the 1920's, there were still important weaknesses in Acción Católica: it could not eliminate the division among Catholics, and often its local leaders were incompetent or out of touch with the social problem. However, under Tedeschini's direction it grew and came to possess tremendous potential. It provided

4. Luis Izaga, S.J., "La iglesia, el régimen político, y los partidos," *Razón y Fe,* 429 (October, 1932), 199-211, realistically faces the problem. He notes that while in theory the church is above politics and has no choice as to form of government as long as the church and the social order are protected, in reality the church is very active in politics, because reason does not always rule political life. When the church is threatened, it will support those parties which offer it protection, but this holds true only for one situation, and does not mean that the church is bound to that party thereafter.

5. See Federico Cardenal Tedeschini, *Discursos y cartas sobre acción católica española,* ed. JDF (Santiago de Compostela, 1958).

the church with the outlines of a powerful organization should the need arise. By 1931, Acción Católica was not large, but its leaders were men in key places.

iv

There remains to be considered the status of the Spanish church in 1931. According to a government census— usually unreliable—of Spain's approximately thirty million population, twenty-three million considered themselves to be Catholics; these figures, however, mean little, for they included the practicing Catholic as well as the nominal Catholic. Geographically, Spain was divided into 9 archdioceses, 53 dioceses, and 20,614 parishes. There were 32,000 secular priests and 7,000 regular priests (members of religious orders), a proportion of 1 to 586 of the population (although this was unevenly distributed; in Andalusia, for example, the ratio was 1 to 1,575). In addition there were some 5,000 nonordained monks, 53,000 nuns, and 13,500 seminarians.[6] In sum, the total ecclesiastical establishment in Spain numbered some 110,-500 persons.

Juridically, the church was established, given privileges, and protected by the state, both under the terms of the concordat of 1851, and the decrees of the council of Trent (1545-63), which were incorporated into the Spanish law. Politically, all archbishops were granted seats in the Senate of the Cortes. In the economic order, ecclesiastical property was perpetually tax-exempt, and the state paid the clergy's salaries. The religious orders provided civil services by working in prisons and municipal hospitals. Each local school board had a church represen-

6. The best sources for these statistics are Vargas Zúñiga's articles in *Razón y Fe*, 462-63 (July-August, 1935), 297; 465 (October, 1935), 153-63. The *Anuario estadístico de España* (1932), pp. 672-73, gives figures from the 1930 census.

tative on it, and the prelates were given the right to inspect all schools. Establishment was extended even to the dead, for the church provided spiritual care for all occupants of state cemeteries, while the state maintained the grounds (which were considered to be church property).

Thus, the church enjoyed a favored position, despite its obvious loss of independence, for the monarch still appointed the higher clergy and the clerical budget was not always proportioned to the cost of living. Whatever the disadvantages of this position, the privileges far outweighed them as far as the majority of the clergy were concerned.

These then were the church's privileges. It is important to clarify the distinction between them and the church's rights. According to Catholic teaching, the church has a right to perform its spiritual functions unhindered by the state. Paramount among these rights is its mission of dispensing the sacraments, and almost as important is its right to direct the education of the faithful. The church's privileges, on the other hand, vary according to time and place. In Spain, they consisted of most of the benefits of establishment—clerical salaries, tax-exempt property, and political representation, among others. Almost consistently throughout history, the church has demanded its rights, and has enjoyed them, even if contrary to the laws of the state. Often it has fought for privileges, but ordinarily it has not counseled civil disobedience to secure them. The fact that many of the clergy and many of the reformers failed to make this distinction between the church's rights and its privileges was to be the cause of much of the conflict between the two factions during the course of the Second Spanish Republic.

By 1931, there can be little doubt that the church had

suffered a moral decline through its alliance with the restoration oligarchy. The anticlerical and antireligious forces found strength in the fact that the church was in a weaker position than ever before in history. Despite this, however, the church was still a power, and it possessed the force of spiritual compulsion over a large sector of the Spanish populace. It was this power that the reformers of the Second Republic were to find so difficult to do away with.

CHAPTER 6

THE CHURCH AND
THE ADVENT OF
THE REPUBLIC

---

i

The dictator resigned in January of 1930 and the Spanish nation embarked upon its most turbulent period in history. The inevitable power vacuum that had attended the demise of every previous dictator was now particularly critical, for the army had lost prestige with the fall of Primo de Rivera. All eyes turned toward the king, who found himself as in 1923 in a tense situation. What would the monarch do?

Alfonso had little choice. On the one hand there was a large and vociferous demand for constitutional government from the democratic liberals and Socialists; on the other the army, the oligarchy, and the church, while interested in rule by law, did not want a revolutionary government that would not only topple them from power but create civil chaos as well. The Rey Caballero knew that their support was the only security against exile. No reputable civilian leader would form a ministry for Alfonso, so careful had the politicians become, and the king had to call in the military again, this time in the person of General Dámaso Berenguer.

Immediate concessions were made to prevent a revolution. Many constitutional rights were restored and there was talk that the government planned elections in the near future. These events gave the opposition forces an opportunity to increase their agitation for a change of regime.

The opposition had become stronger during the dictatorship. The Socialist party, led by the general secretary of the UGT, Francisco Largo Caballero, numbered almost 250,000 members. They, along with the anarcho-syndicalists, desired not only legal restrictions on the church but envisioned the ultimate elimination of religion in Spain. The anarcho-syndicalists had almost four times as many members as the Socialists but were not so well organized politically. The democratic liberals, all anticlerical, and now republican, were represented by many political parties. The left democratic liberals were the most numerous; their emerging leader was Manuel Azaña. The right democratic liberals, not as strong, had not yet developed a leader. Another left group, the Radical Socialist party, was rapidly gaining adherents, but had no strong leader either. Finally, there was a right-center party, the Radicals. Its leader, once a fiery anticlerical but now grown corrupt and conservative, was Alejandro Lerroux. Most of these opposition parties were represented on a smaller scale within the various regional movements, Catalan, Basque, and Galician; their primary aim was local autonomy, and only secondarily did they support national interests.

The monarchy's supporters were somewhat less numerous, but they were very strong. There were three monarchist groups: the Alfonsists, who wanted the king to rule without any change; the constitutional monarchists, who wanted Alfonso to abdicate in favor of an heir who would govern constitutionally; and the Carlists, who, while carrying the banner for the pretender, Jaime, preferred Alfonso to a republic. These three groups were also represented on a smaller scale within the regional movements; generally, however, they could be counted on to place their allegiance to the king before their provincial loyalty.

Despite the growing strength of the opposition the political situation was still fluid. Had the king been aware and responsible, effective political and social reforms could have stemmed the demands for a republic. But not since Charles III had a Spanish Bourbon shown political awareness. The king did nothing and the clamor for change grew.

The episcopate viewed the political situation with increasing apprehension. Should it continue to support the king, or should it proclaim neutrality so that its position could be somewhat salvaged if the regime were overthrown? Unfortunately for the episcopate, the ranking prince of the Spanish church, Pedro Cardinal Segura y Sáenz, Archbishop of Toledo, was not only a close friend of Alfonso but also a headstrong man whose second nature was opposition to any nonmonarchical group. Segura, whose vigorous appearance belied his fifty years, had greatly impressed the king, and in six years the cardinal had risen from the small bishopric of Coria in Extremadura to the archbishopric of Toledo and the Primacy of the Spanish Church. Perhaps this promotion accounted for the primate's strong attachment to Alfonso and the monarchy. In any event, Segura lived a frugal life in his palace at Toledo, was considered a good churchman and scholar, and was well known for his social and humanitarian labors. However, he was out of touch with the political realities of the twentieth century; this, combined with a singular gift for displaying obstinate firmness when moderate conciliation was needed conspired to bring about a chain of circumstances fatal for the church.[1]

The cardinal-primate responded to the political situation with a pastoral letter to Spanish Catholics on February 27, 1930.[2] Outlining the political obligation of Spain's Catholics, he reviewed papal thought, citing Pius X's *Inter Catholicos Hispanae* and two statements of Pope Pius XI. In 1924, Segura noted, Pius had justified the role of the papacy in politics, declaring that: "The Holy Father should not concern himself with politics, but when politics touches the altar . . . not only do I have a right, but I have an obligation to give indications and norms to Catholics, who have a right to ask for and an obligation to follow my [advice]." And, on November 6, 1929, the Pope had stated that Spanish Catholics could belong to or organize any political party as long as it respected the church's rights and was not of a "revolutionary character."

Segura also defended Acción Católica, denying that the organization was being used as a pretext to hide the church's political activities. However, he reaffirmed the church's right to enter politics should it be threatened. The primate concluded his pastoral by declaring that Catholics had an absolute obligation to obey the norms established by the church.

Other clergymen supported these views during the early months of 1930. Monsignor Isidro Gomá y Tomás,

1. Ramos-Oliviera, *Politics, Economics and Men*, p. 438, says Segura was "a good example of a thirteenth century churchman, and a glaring anachronism in 1931, even in Spain."

2. In *El Siglo Futuro* (Madrid), March 10, 1930.

Bishop of Tarrazona, stated that Catholics had an obligation to support political parties and politicians pledged to
defend the church's rights. Clarifying this statement, he
adamantly condemned socialism as being the antithesis of
Catholicism.[3]

Essentially, the prelates' concern was prompted by
their position. The background of disorder and anticlerical vindictiveness of nineteenth-century republicanism
confirmed them in support of the monarchy. Although
most were convinced monarchists, being appointees of the
king, their active political opposition to the republicans
was not based primarily upon an attachment to monarchical
government *per se*. The bishops were motivated by the sure
knowledge that a republican government would act
against the church. Their situation was difficult, if not
desperate, for they could not support any movement
avowedly determined to decrease not only their privileges but also to do away with their rights. Thus, the
episcopate was driven to a more extreme support of the
monarchy and its institutions—unwisely to be sure, but
neutrality offered only hope with no assurances, and support of republicanism was suicide. As a result, the republicans, with some justification, lumped the church together with the army and the oligarchy in their attacks
upon the monarchy.

ii

Meanwhile, during this first half of 1930, the republican parties were gaining adherents and consolidating
their positions. Among the various parties, leaders were
moving to positions of power. One of the most prominent
was Niceto Alcalá Zamora, a man destined to personify

3. "Los deberes cristianos de patria" (March 13, 1930), in Isidro
Cardenal Gomá y Tomás, *Antilaicismo* (Barcelona, 1935), II, 53-102.

the dilemma of the Catholic republican. Alcalá Zamora was a fifty-four-year-old Andalusian lawyer with a fairly undistinguished political career. Elected to the Cortes in 1905 from one of the most *cacique*-ridden provinces of Spain, he had held unimportant portfolios in the ministries of 1917 and 1922. Still a monarchist in 1929, Alcalá Zamora had become a vocal opponent of the dictatorship and had rallied a small conservative group around him. He was a practicing Catholic but an anticlerical.[4]

Alcalá Zamora declared his conversion to republicanism three months after Primo de Rivera's fall. At Valencia, he stated that he was in favor of a conservative republic that would not disfavor any group, even the monarchists. As for the church, he proposed that the clergy should retain their representation in the upper chamber of the Cortes. "With the Archbishop of Valencia [represented, you ask me?] . . . With the Cardinal of Toledo [as President of the Senate] if you wish. . . ."[5]

By July, 1930, the monarchist-turned-republican had gathered together a group of like-minded politicians, and they formed the Right Liberal Republican party. In a manifesto they called for complete religious liberty and the gradual and cordial separation of church and state. Alcalá Zamora's recent conversion to republicanism was not lost upon the more extreme republicans. They saw that his Catholicism and moderation would attract the support of those Catholics who were republican in sympathy but who feared radical attacks upon religion. Simply stated, the presence of Alcalá Zamora in a republican

4. Ramos-Oliviera, *Politics, Economics and Men*, p. 267, says of him: ". . . his ambition was vanity; his elegance artifice; his talent dexterity; his Catholicism superstition."

5. From a speech at the Teatro Apolo, April 13, 1930, as quoted in Joaquín Arrarás Iribarren, *Historia de la segunda república española* (Madrid, 1956), I, 29. Most of the speech was censored in the Spanish press; see *Informaciones* (Madrid), April 15, 1930.

government would be an assurance of both political and religious moderation. Accordingly, the other republican leaders asked Alcalá Zamora to join them in signing the pact of San Sebastián (August, 1930), a manifesto calling for a return to constitutional government. The signers, now the strong nucleus of the republican movement included, among others, Manuel Azaña, Alejandro Lerroux, Álvaro de Albornoz, Marcelino Domingo, Diego Martínez Barrios, Santiago Casares Quiroga, and Miguel Maura. Of these, only Alcalá Zamora and Maura were practicing Catholics; all were anticlerical.

The revolutionary movement gathered momentum. In September, a republican rally was held in Madrid and Azaña assured the spectators that the minimum religious program of the revolutionary committee (the signers of the pact of San Sebastián) was complete liberty of conscience.[6] Throughout these months, the republicans said little about the church, for they needed the support of all the people of Spain and could ill afford to antagonize so diversified a group as the Catholics.

During the winter of 1930-31, revolutionary agitation increased. There was industrial violence in the provinces where the anarchists were strong. Two uprisings occurred in December, and both were put down by the government. As a result, two minor revolutionaries were executed and the revolutionary committee was arrested and imprisoned. Indignation swept the country and many prominent persons came to the defense of the incarcerated committee. This time the king was forced to give in to the nation's demands. The government proposed a series of elections for a new Cortes. To test public sentiment the first election was to be for municipal offices only and

6. Speech of September 29, 1930, at the Plaza de Toros, from Manuel Azaña, *Una política, 1930-1932* (Madrid, 1932), p. 27.

was scheduled for April 12, 1931. Complete constitutional guarantees were restored and the revolutionary committee was released from prison in time to begin campaigning actively. All stood for office.

Although the committee had no idea that the election would result in a change of regime, some members began to think of the problems of governing. Alcalá Zamora and Maura were particularly interested in formulating a religious policy that would be compatible with their beliefs and at the same time satisfy the more extreme members of the committee. Above all, the two Catholics did not want to endanger a new government by antagonizing the church. To this end, Maura approached a well-known republican writer on politico-religious problems, Jaime Torrubiano Ripoll, and asked him to advise the committee.

Torrubiano Ripoll—an excommunicate—cautioned against the dangers of clericalism and warned that a new government could not rid itself of these threats simply by legislating against the church. Instead, a strong and workable social program that could attract the support of moderate Catholics and workers should be the cornerstone of any new regime. He advised against granting the franchise to women, for they could too easily become the tools of the clergy. A concordat should be negotiated with the Holy See, for this would attract Catholic support to any regime. Torrubiano Ripoll emphasized that moderation should be the committee's guiding policy toward the church, since Spanish history taught that church support or at least church neutrality was a *sine qua non* for the lasting stability of any regime.[7] The soundness of this advice was to be fully demonstrated by later events.

7. See Jaime Torrubiano Ripoll, *Política religiosa de la democracia española* (Madrid, 1933).

iii

The municipal elections of 1931 were the first elections in over eight years. Although the republicans had little hope of overthrowing the monarchy, they decided to campaign for the establishment of a republic, using the elections as a show of strength. The electoral laws were more favorable to bloc voting, and the republicans allied with the Socialists to form a coalition including all of the opposition parties except the anarcho-syndicalists. The latter refused to join in political action to achieve their aims, but their press supported the coalition. The monarchists also formed a coalition in support of the regime, however they were unable to include some splinter groups within it.

The nature of the Republican-Socialist coalition made agreement on a religious platform difficult—as indeed it made agreement on most questions difficult, if not impossible. For, it was apparent from the beginning that the Socialists envisioned any republican regime as a means toward the implantation of a classless society, while the republicans viewed the establishment of a republic as an end in itself. This fundamental difference stood in the way of a practical solution of the religious problem.

The position of the Socialist party was clear. For years it had been calling for disestablishment and the regulation of the church's political and social powers. The Socialist approach to the religious problem was simple: the monarchy was the cause of all Spain's troubles; whoever made common cause with it was an enemy of the people and would be dealt with accordingly.

On the other hand, the republicans—right, left, and center—had to play a dual role on the religious question. In order to hold the coalition together they had to give some assurance to the Socialists that they would not oppose strong action against the church. At the same time, the republicans had to promise Catholic republicans that the church would not be persecuted. Because the republicans represented all shades of opinion on the church question, from the extreme anti-Catholicism of Álvaro de Albornoz, the Radical Socialist leader, to the conservative anticlericalism of Alcalá Zamora, the only religious group they could attack with agreement and impunity was the episcopate. A manifesto by three of Spain's leading intellectuals, Gregorio Marañón, Ramón Pérez de Ayala, and José Ortega y Gassett expressed this attitude. The three declared that the monarchy had been nothing more than the "manager of a mutual aid society composed of the higher clergy—not the humble clergy or the popular religious orders—, the big bankers . . . [and] the military. . . ."[8]

As the campaign became more intense, the Republican-Socialist coalition made an appeal for the support of those Catholics who wanted an assurance of security for religion. A manifesto published four days before the elections stated: "Catholics: the maximum program of the [Republican-Socialist] coalition is freedom of religion. . . . Only religious liberty can emancipate us from discreditable clericalism. . . . The Republic . . . will not persecute any religion. Tolerance will be its theme."[9]

Apparently, many Catholics were attracted to the coalition and not a few priests openly sympathized with the republicans. In some quarters, the church's official statements were moderate. The Bishop of Tuy, in a pastoral published April 4, noted that Catholics had an obligation to vote for those who promised to work for the "better

8. *El Liberal* (Madrid), April 10, 1931.
9. *Ibid.*, April 8, 1931.

interests of God and country," but he named no political parties.[10]

Others among the clergy were more extreme and some still tended to the thesis that church and monarchy were consubstantial. In a book published immediately before the campaign began, Father Hilario Yaben, the lectoral canon of Siguenza, defended the monarchy and warned that Spanish republican movements had always been anticlerical and that there was no basis for thinking that a republic would respect the church's rights.[11] An article in the Jesuit publication, *Razón y Fe,* observed that even the most moderate republican position (Alcalá Zamora's) on the religious question was contrary to Catholic doctrine and noted that "anti-Catholic fury is always the muse of Spanish Republicanism."[12]

The two leading Catholic newspapers, the Traditionalist *El Siglo Futuro* and the moderate *El Debate,* supported the monarchists.[13] *El Debate's* tone, however, was mild. Its editor, Ángel Herrera Oria, reviewed papal pronouncements on elections, noting that attacks upon constituted governments were illicit, as all power came from God. At the same time, Herrera Oria also observed that

10. *El Debate* (Madrid), April 4, 1931.

11. *Monarquía o república?* (Madrid, 1931).

12. "La última crísis política en España" (unsigned), *Razón y Fe,* 408 (March 25, 1931), 536-53.

13. *El Siglo Futuro* had been founded at the turn of the century by Ramón Nocedal to defend his Integrist position. It had scarcely changed its views since that time. It called for a return to an absolute monarchy and a privileged position for the church, with no religious toleration. It obeyed the teachings of the church but did not consider the Pope's views sufficiently Catholic. *El Debate* was owned and edited by Ángel Herrera Oria, who bought the paper in 1915 with capital supplied by "Bilbao financiers, the Bishop of Madrid, and several people close to the Jesuits" (Henry W. Buckley, *Life and Death of the Spanish Republic* [London, 1940], p. 106). It normally served as a sounding board for moderate Catholic views, while *El Siglo Futuro* was popularly considered to voice the opinions of Cardinal Segura.

the church had no choice as to form of government and that it could live with any regime as long as the "church's rights be respected."[14] While his views could be implied to mean that moderate Catholics would not support the republicans, he made it clear that if a republic were established, neither would they support a counterrevolution.

Until late in the campaign the church's stand could be interpreted in many ways. At least, Catholics could decide for themselves which of the candidates, even within the Republican-Socialist coalition, would safeguard their religious rights. This period of grace ended and the issue took on new meaning when the Bishop of Vitoria, Monsignor Mateo Múgica, set forth the electoral obligations of the faithful of his diocese in a pastoral letter published April 9.[15]

Bishop Múgica left no doubts concerning those obligations. He specifically stated that Catholics could not licitly vote for any Republican-Socialist candidate. Neither could they vote for one of the dissident rightist groups not in the monarchist coalition. Compounding the dilemma for Catholic republicans, Múgica said that no Catholic could abdicate his responsibility and abstain from voting. In other words, the Bishop told the faithful of Vitoria that they would be placing their souls in mortal danger if they did not vote for the monarchist coalition.

Múgica's pastoral was not so much a religious blunder as a political one, for the church had long been accustomed to dictating the political obligations of Catholics. The historian, gifted with hindsight, can view Múgica's pastoral as the first in a long series of overt clerical opposition against the Republic, but the Bishop of Vitoria

14. *El Debate*, March 31, 1931.
15. *El Siglo Futuro*, April 9, 1931.

certainly expected none of the consequences that were to follow. For him, the political question was reduced simply to the question of the survival of the church in Spain. Although there was some justification for his views in the light of later events, it would be difficult to determine his own culpability for those actions against the church.

In any event, the pastoral was a provocation, and the Republicans forgot their position of balance. *El Liberal,* the principal anticlerical paper, noted that, although good clergymen had been republicans "since 1812 [sic], there is now the dissident voice of the Bishop of Vitoria, who has no scruples in placing the Episcopate in a bad light." Even the king, it observed, had denied that church and monarchy were consubstantial (in a speech in Rome in 1923). "Thus we have the case of some Spanish clericals who, usually more papist than the Pope, [now] are more monarchist than the King."[16] Reaction to the pastoral was heard from all quarters. The dean of Spanish intellectuals, Miguel de Unamuno, commented that the church was making a grave mistake by meddling in politics and if a democratic regime did offend the church, the latter would not be blameless.[17]

Just as eagerly, the Catholic press came to Múgica's defense. *El Siglo Futuro* praised the bishop and declared that the only real choice in the campaign was monarchy or anarchy.[18] *El Debate* left its moderate position and published the "ten commandments of the voter," one of which was that no Catholic could vote, at that time, for any Republican-Socialist candidate.[19] Both papers warned of the dangers of republican anticlericalism and noted

16. April 9, 1931.
17. *El Sol* (Madrid), April 11, 1931.
18. April 9, 1931.
19. April 10, 1931.

that scurrilous pamphlets predicting action against the church were being circulated in the larger towns.

On Sunday, April 12, the electorate went to the polls, and the religious question was largely forgotten because of the surprising election results. The monarchists won a majority of the municipalities throughout the nation, but forty-six of the fifty largest towns voted republican. As the rural vote was still largely controlled by the *caciques,* only the urban vote could be counted as a true mandate of public opinion. The Republican-Socialists had won more than they had hoped for and they began immediate agitation for the establishment of a republic. On April 13 the king's ministers, led by the Conde de Romanones, leader of the constitutional monarchists, asked Alfonso to abdicate his throne to prevent bloodshed. The king refused to abdicate but agreed to leave the country.

In the late afternoon of April 14, 1931, the Second Spanish Republic was proclaimed amid orderly rejoicing throughout the country. Contrary to Spanish tradition, no blood was spilled and no churches were burned.

CHAPTER 7

ATTEMPTS AT CONCILIATION
AND THE OUTBREAK
OF HOSTILITIES

The Second Spanish Republic was from its inception plagued with problems for which no practical solution was ever reached. The chief impediment to its stability was the threat posed by extremists of both right and left. At one extreme, a large group of disgruntled monarchists desired the return of the monarchy and the predominance of the church, army, and oligarchy. On the other, the anarcho-syndicalists wanted immediate radical reforms as a prelude to proletarian rule. The regionalists also wanted concessions. The Catalans had enthusiastically taken advantage of the monarchy's collapse to proclaim the Independent Catalan State. Alcalá Zamora, as president of the provisional government, made a hurried trip to Barcelona to lead them back to the fold without hurting their pride.

Despite these problems—perhaps because of their enormity—the government's immediate concern was the religious problem. If a solution acceptable to the church could be reached the cohesiveness of the extreme right would be broken, and the republic would stand upon firmer ground.

i

The provisional government of the republic was composed of members of the revolutionary committee. Three of the new ministers had important roles in the realm of church-state relations: Fernando de los Ríos, minister of justice, Alejandro Lerroux, foreign minister, and Miguel Maura, home minister.

Fernando de los Ríos was a professor of law, one of the outstanding intellectuals of the Socialist party and the chief heir of the Krausistas. Imposing of mien, resembling a bearded nineteenth-century visionary, he termed himself a "humanistic socialist"—which meant a belief in evolutionary methods and the idea that a viable socialism would be more worthy for its cultural uplifting rather than for its class leveling. He displayed no spirit of rancor towards the church, but he wanted its social, political, and intellectual grip on the nation loosened. As minister of justice, he was charged with dispensing the clerical budget and ruling on church-state affairs.

Alejandro Lerroux, a sixty-seven-year-old journalist, was the founder and leader of the Radical party. As a younger man he had been violently anticlerical, one of the *provocateurs* of the *semana trágica,* and his Radicals had been truly radical. However, since 1909 the Radicals had drifted to center-conservatism, having been the official opposition party for so long. Lerroux was known popularly as the "Emperor of the Paralelo" (the red-light district of Barcelona), and there were rumors concerning his rather sudden acquisition of wealth in the last few years. The history of Lerroux's career left the general impression that he could be bought with promises of wealth or power, and thus, his position on the church question was, to put it mildly, flexible. He was skilled in parliamentary discourse and appeared to be an able administrator. As foreign minister, his charge was negotiating with the Holy See.

Miguel Maura was the only practicing Catholic in the ministry besides Alcalá Zamora. A lawyer and the son of a prime minister, he was a recent convert to republicanism. Politically, he resembled Alcalá Zamora—he also had been selected by the revolutionary committee because of his Catholicism and moderation. He differed from the president in that Maura was an honest man and not prepared to sacrifice principles for power. His responsibility as home minister was the protection of the church, as of all persons and institutions, from violent and illegal actions.

Lerroux, De los Ríos, and Maura, with the other members of the government, signed the Juridical Statute of April 14, a statement of its aims. Section 3 of the statute declared: "The Provisional Government . . . [will] fully respect the individual's conscience. [It decrees] freedom of religion. . . . At no time can the State ask the citizen to reveal his religious convictions."[1] The government then began negotiating with the Holy See, because even this mild decree infringed upon the concordat of 1851.

From April 15 to May 9, daily meetings were held in Madrid between a government negotiating team and representatives of the Holy See. The discussions centered around the civil status of the church in Spain. Alcalá

1. Published April 15, 1931, in *La Gaceta de Madrid*. At the same time, the government ordered all civil governors to refrain from attending religious services in an official capacity and cautioned them to have only courteous relations with the clergy.

Zamora and the other moderates in the government were hopeful of reaching an understanding that would win church support for the republic, thereby eliminating any clerical threat to its stability. For its part, the Holy See wanted assurances of safety and protection for the church. In these negotiations, the Holy See was represented by one of its most astute and likeable diplomats, the Italian who had been nuncio to Spain since 1921, Monsignor Federico Tedeschini, titular Archbishop of Lepanto.

Tall and graceful, with the honest round face of a central Italian, the fifty-eight-year-old nuncio was, in a sense, a refugee from Italy. In his earlier years, he had been an ardent supporter of Don Luigi Sturzo, the leader of Italian Christian Democracy, whose party had crumbled before Mussolini's Blackshirts in 1923. Pope Benedict XV, perhaps sensing Tedeschini's uneasiness with the Italian situation, sent him to Madrid as nuncio. Tedeschini's main task before the fall of the monarchy had been to rebuild Acción Católica; now it was to avert an open break with the republic. The nuncio realized, as did everyone concerned with the situation, that the republic would act in some way against the church. His job was to soften the blow as much as possible. Thus, he was disposed to grant many concessions, and to close his eyes to anticlerical violence, as long as there was some hope of reconciliation with the republic. It is a monument to Tedeschini's skill that during his tenure as nuncio the Vatican never broke diplomatic relations with the republic.

Tedeschini's relations with some members of the Spanish episcopate were not cordial. In particular, he and Cardinal Segura did not get alone. Much of this hostility was the normal antagonism that would exist between any primate and a papal representative; but beyond this,

Segura found the nuncio too advanced and too conciliatory, while Tedeschini considered the primate to be one of the main stumbling blocks to an efficient and aware national church.

Nevertheless, despite Tedeschini's personal feelings, he still was bound to the position of the Holy See. Vatican policy was, of course, primarily formulated by Pope Pius XI (Achille Ratti). The Pontiff was a man who knew the world. Politically, his pontificate had been dominated by a conciliatory policy, for Pius had been forced to deal with the many territorial and political changes resulting from World War I. The Pope's most important diplomatic victory had been the settlement of the sixty-year-old Roman question by the Lateran Treaties with Mussolini in 1929. In his relations with foreign powers, Pius pursued two goals: the interests of the church, and the peace that was essential for the church to fulfill its mission.

Under the Pope was the Curia, the administrative staff of the Vatican. The two—Pope and Curia—did not always have the same ideas or the same policy. Being composed of cardinals from many nations, the Curia was more conservative and more disposed to letting the bishops of each country pursue their own policy in national affairs. In 1931, the most important member of the Curia was the Papal Secretary of State, Eugenio Cardinal Pacelli, scion of an aristocratic Roman family.

The Holy See's policy toward Spain was conditioned by the knowledge that the government was in anticlerical hands and would likely stay that way for some time to come. The only logical policy was to maintain cordial relations in the hope that the republic would not legislate too harshly against the church. No legal safeguards protecting the church could be formulated at that time. A new concordat or formal *modus vivendi* could not be possible until a Cortes was elected. The provisional government had no mandate to negotiate one, and the Pope did not want to experience another broken accord, for he was already working on his encyclical, *Non Abbiamo Bisogno* (June, 1931), protesting Il Duce's violation of the two-year-old Lateran Pact.

Therefore, Tedeschini did not demand a formal agreement with the government. He wanted simply an assurance, which he got. Alcalá Zamora and Lerroux promised him that the provisional government would honor all international agreements contracted by the monarchy (this meant the 1851 concordat) and that both men would work to prevent the enactment of any antireligious (not anticlerical) clauses in the draft of the new constitution. In return, the nuncio promised to use his influence to get the Spanish clergy's acceptance of the republic.

The third member of the government's negotiating committee, De los Ríos, gave no assurances. He said that nothing could be done until a constitution was formulated.[2] De los Ríos' attitude expressed a common feeling among the more radical Republicans. They were waiting until the new Cortes should legislate against the church; then, they would present the Holy See with a juridical *fait accompli* and hope to work out a *modus vivendi* on that basis—an approach which, as Ramos-Oliviera notes, not even the French Republicans in their most anticlerical days would have attempted.[3]

2. United States State Department Dispatch 344, Ambassador Irwin B. Laughlin to Secretary of State Henry L. Stimson, April 23, 1931 (752.66A/1). All State Department communications hereafter cited as S.D.

3. *Politics, Economics and Men*, p. 447.

ii

Tedeschini evidently fulfilled his part of the bargain, at least in regard to some of the bishops, for within a week after the proclamation of the republic, a number of pastoral letters and circulars appeared. All were addressed to the clergy, who were advised to refrain from political activity and to show their allegiance to the government by cooperating with the civil authorities.[4] At the same time, most of the bishops were preparing pastorals, sermons, statements, and circulars addressed to the laity, although these were not published until early May.

In general, the second round of statements directed the laity to obey the government, not as an act of political expediency, but as an obligation of conscience. The views of Eustaquio Cardinal Ilundáin y Esteban, Archbishop of Seville, were typical. He stated that Catholics should support the government because Christian prudence prompted such support and because the Holy See desired them to. Even the staunch monarchist Bishop Múgica told the faithful of Vitoria to respect the government and asked for prayers to illuminate it in its dealings with the church.[5]

For the most part, the government followed a hands-off policy toward the church throughout the rest of April. Some anticlerical incidents occurred, but the government frowned upon actions of this sort. Apparently, moderates in both church and government were in control of policy. However, in early May, the government started moving against the church, evidently because of rumors that the

4. For example, see the letter of Monsignor Manuel Irurita Almández, Bishop of Barcelona, in *A.B.C.* (Madrid), April 21, 1931.

5. Cardinal Ilundáin's pastoral is in the *Boletín Oficial Eclesiástico del Arzobispado de Sevilla*, May 2, 1931, pp. 179-84; Bishop Múgica's circular is in the *Boletín Eclesiástico del Obispado de Vitoria*, May 1, 1931, p. 330.

church was planning to liquidate some of its investments. On May 2, despite earlier announcements that the government had no intention of confiscating the church's possessions, De los Ríos issued a decree prohibiting the sale or transferal of church property. The extremists were getting the upper hand in the government. Would the extremists in the church take over?

The answer to this question hinged on Cardinal Segura's plans. The primate had a great amount of power and influence, and his monarchist leanings were known to all. At first, Segura remained silent despite attacks from the leftist press. A report published in all the newspapers claimed that the cardinal had thundered: "May the wrath of God . . . descend upon Spain if the Republic should persevere."[6]

The Catholic press denied the report, but the leftist papers continued their attacks, and the government placed credence in them. The minister of justice delivered a note to the nuncio complaining that "the government has received contradictory views concerning the statements of the Cardinal-Primate. . . . In view of this . . . the Nuncio is informed that the [Government] is sure that Rome will not permit this attack upon the constituted power."[7]

How long would the primate remain officially silent? Could the nuncio influence Segura to pursue a moderate course? Segura answered both these questions on May 6, in a pastoral letter directed to Spain's Catholics, his first official statement since the foundation of the republic.

The cardinal reviewed papal thought in regard to constituted powers, but in much more militant language than the other prelates used. Whereas they had hoped and prayed that the government would respect the church's

6. *El Socialista* (Madrid), April 23, 1931, among others.
7. *El Debate,* April 26, 1931.

rights, the primate assumed that it would not. He stressed the gravity of the moment for Spain, and directed Catholics to follow the attitude of the Holy See in giving respect and obedience to the government, for the common good.

The most important part of Segura's pastoral was devoted to a review of the history of church-state relations. He pointed out that the monarchy had helped the church in working together for the peace of the country. The primate expressed a debt of gratitude to Alfonso XIII: "Who can forget his devotion to the Holy See, and that it was he who consecrated Spain to the Sacred Heart?" Segura noted that he himself had suffered grave injuries and calumnies, and ended the pastoral declaring that "we have not talked of monarchy or republic, but only of the [coming] election campaign. . . . This is not a time of discussion; rather it is one of work, prayer, and sacrifice."[8] Like Múgica's pre-election pastoral Segura's statements were unfortunate. Although many of his contentions were true, it was not so much what the cardinal said as how he said it. At the very least, the primate lacked prudence, however much his courage may be admitted. Events followed quickly.

The government protested the pastoral almost immediately. De los Ríos delivered a note to the nuncio demanding Segura's recall. In a public statement, the minister of justice commented that the matter was grave and that the government would not allow itself to be attacked in this manner again. He declared: "[Segura's] pastoral is plain interference by the Church in politics. . . . The Government desires to treat the question of separation of Church and State on a plane of respectful cordiality, but

8. In *El Siglo Futuro*, May 6, 1931.

the tone and character of the Cardinal's document make this task extremely difficult."[9]

Then, the government acted, touching the church's most sensitive spot—education. On the same day the pastoral was published, a decree ended obligatory religious education in the state schools and made it voluntary on the request of the parents.[10] In answer, the Spanish episcopate signed a collective pastoral at Toledo. The bishops hoped that the provisional government would "honor the Church's rights, as promised."[11] These actions were overshadowed by the fateful events of the next few days.

iii

On Sunday morning, May 10, strollers on the Calle del Alcalá in Madrid were surprised to hear the strains of the "Royal March" drifting out of a second-floor window. People gathered outside the building and murmurings of indignation were heard in the street. After all, these were the halcyon days of a *la bonita república,* and to most Spaniards the preceding month had been one of pleasant if unnatural serenity. Thus it came as somewhat of a shock to realize that there were people in Spain who desired a return of the monarchy. Of course, the grand dukes and the *gente de dinero* were known monarchists, but it was assumed they would confine their reminiscing to their private clubs and *tertulias* rather than blatantly display their political affiliations to the Madrid populace.

The monarchists inside the building were meeting for a precise political purpose. The government had recently announced that elections for a Constituent Cortes would be held in late June, and the royalists were gather-

9. *El Sol,* May 9, 1931.
10. Soto de Gongoiti, *La iglesia católica y el estado español,* p. 133.
11. Signed May 9, published in the *Boletín Oficial Eclesiástico del Arzobispado de Toledo,* May 16, 1931, pp. 153-55.

ing to organize their campaign. The meeting had been well publicized in the monarchist press, but notwithstanding, the crowd outside felt that the royalists should have confined their activities behind closed doors. Even worse, as people gathered, a young man appeared on the balcony and in a moment of exultation, shouted, "Viva el Rey!" The murmurs of the crowd below turned to shouts and cries of "Viva la República!"

At this moment, a taxi drew up to the building and two well-known monarchists got out. The cabdriver turned to them and began a political argument. A scuffle ensued, and the royalists, after rapping the cabdriver smartly on the head, pushed their way through the crowd and into the building. The rumor quickly spread that the taxi driver had been killed (he was not even wounded), and the crowd began tearing up the pavement and hurling stones at the building.

By this time the civil guard had arrived. They moved the crowd back and evacuated the monarchists. However, the guard was unable to prevent the mob from overturning and burning the royalists' automobiles that were parked nearby.

The mob then moved on to the Castellana and the offices of *A.B.C.*, the monarchist newspaper. On the way, they sacked one of *El Debate*'s newspaper kiosks. Clearly, they were in an ugly mood. The staff inside the offices of *A.B.C.* closed the shutters, but the mob had come prepared; they had brought cans of gasoline, with which they soaked the base of the building. Once again, the civil guard arrived in time to prevent a fire. In the scuffle that followed, someone from within the building fired shots, killing one person and wounding a few others. However, the guard dispersed the mob, and an uneasy calm prevailed in Madrid.

The ministry was concerned, and it took immediate action. That evening Maura announced the suspension of *A.B.C.*, and *El Debate* in an effort to prevent further provocations. When the ministry met, Maura informed it that there were rumors that a general strike was to be called the next morning and that there were plans afoot to burn the churches. Certainly the latter was no secret, for at that moment agitators were haranguing crowds in the Puerta del Sol, calling for the churches to go up in flames. Maura asked the other ministers for emergency powers— the calling out of the army—to prevent disorder. They refused.[12]

The next morning, workers arriving at their jobs heard that a general strike had been called. UGT headquarters quickly countered by ordering its members to stay at their jobs to show their faith in the republic. The UGT knew of the plans to burn the churches and they wanted none of their members implicated. Furthermore, if the anarchists were behind the agitation, the Socialists were perfectly willing to let them take full blame for any church burnings. This way the country would see that the Socialists were not disposed to achieving their aims by violence. Simply stated, the Socialists had a vested interest in the republic and although they viewed it as a means to an end, those means were necessary and had to be preserved.

At 10:30 A.M., a group of young men carrying cans of gasoline appeared outside the Jesuit church and *convento* of San Francisco Borja on the Gran Vía. First, they tore up the paving and began throwing rocks at the building. Then, they poured gasoline on the structure and touched off a fire. As the fire started, the burners entered through

12. Maura revealed this in a speech on January 10, 1932, in the Cine de la Ópera, Madrid, as reported in *El Liberal*, January 12, 1932. None of the leftist papers questioned Maura's veracity.

a side door, drove out the clergy, and sacked both buildings. As the church went up in flames, the people of Madrid were attracted and a crowd gathered. The firemen
were called, but when they arrived, some persons in the
crowd threatened them and warned them not to put
out the flames. The firemen then joined the rest of the
crowd in watching the spectacle impassively. The civil
guard did not appear.

After this, the same group of young men moved on
and the pattern was repeated at the Carmelite church on
the Plaza de España. In rapid succession, the Jesuit
church and college on the Calle del Alberto Aguilera, the
Christian Brothers *convento* on the Calle del Bravo
Murillo and the Bernadine *convento* in Vallecas were
sacked and burned. Within three hours, the disorders had
spread to the suburbs and the Mercedarian *convento* and
parish church of Bellas Vistas, both in Cuatro Caminos,
the Salesian college on Villamíl, and the Sacred Heart
college and Jesuit college, both in Chamartín, were
assaulted.

The ministry had met immediately after the report of
the first burning. Maura told the other ministers he was
going to call out the guard and the army to protect the
rest of the churches, and he wanted them to countersign
his orders. They refused. Reportedly, one of the ministers told him, "All the *conventos* in Spain are not worth
the life of a single republican." Maura then offered to
resign his post, but the other ministers refused to accept
his resignation, and they persuaded him to stay on.
Maura did, probably because he felt that if he could keep
pressuring the ministers, eventually they would give in;
without him, who knew how long the ministry would remain inactive?

Therefore, after the first burning, orders were sent to

the firemen and the guard that they were to arrest no one nor attempt to extinguish the fires until the crowds had dispersed. Not until 2:00 P.M. did the ministry begin to realize the effects of their inaction. By this time the burnings were getting out of hand and were spreading rapidly —if this kept up, would not the church be justified in revolting against the government before the day was over? Maura and the more moderate ministers finally succeeded in prevailing upon the majority to stop the disorders. At 2:00, troops under the command of General Quiepo de Llano were ordered out, and martial law was declared in Madrid.

The army went into action immediately and although attempts were made to burn other churches, the incendiaries were dispersed. None, however, was arrested. Peace, along with a thick cloud of smoke, fell over the city at nightfall.

If Madrid was at peace, southern Spain was not. By evening, the news of the burnings had spread to the provinces, and as if by prearranged plan, churches and *conventos* were attacked throughout southern Spain. Málaga experienced an evening of terror, for the whole proletarian populace joined in burning forty-one religious buildings including the bishop's palace; only one out of eleven parish churches was left untouched. In Seville four churches and *conventos* were burned; Cádiz had four; Jerez de la Frontera, five; Algeciras, two; Sanlúcar de Barrameda, two; Alicante, thirteen; Murcia, four; and Valencia had a total of twenty-one assaults before the evening was over.

Most of the disorders in the provinces followed the precedents established in Madrid, with the civil guard and firemen watching impassively, although they were under orders from Madrid to prevent the attacks. The army had to be called out, and it was not until four days later, on May 15, that the government was able to announce officially that the incendiarism had been stopped.

As the smoke of a hundred burning churches hung over Spain, questions were asked. Who was responsible? Although the Communists proudly announced that they had burned the churches, their claim was not taken seriously.[13] The Spanish Communist party was small, and it was apparent that they were trying, unwisely, to reap the benefits of the burnings—i.e., they would appear to the working classes as true Spanish revolutionaries, with much more courage and strength than they actually had. No other group admitted responsibility. None of the incendiaries had been arrested, and only later did some of the stolen objects appear, in the hands of common criminals.

It appears then that the burnings had been planned. With the possible exception of Málaga, where a great degree of spontaneity was evident, the fires had been the work of about a hundred men in each town. All were armed and carrying gasoline. The burners were familiar with the interiors of the churches and *conventos*; they made rapid work of sacking them, and the more precious items were stolen. None of the clergy was killed, for the burners had made certain that the buildings were evacuated before they were destroyed. This pattern points to a skillful plot; certainly the burnings were not the spontaneous anticlerical violence of the mob.

Whoever planned the burnings did so to discredit the government. The plotters assumed that the ministry would not risk damaging the government's popularity with the people by arresting the burners or by forcing the crowd to let the firemen put out the flames. Although the premises of this assumption were false—for the crowd was

13. *Informaciones,* May 12, 1931.

impassive and probably would not have hindered the firemen in their work—the plotters judged the ministry's reaction successfully. At the same time, the burners did not want to provoke a clerical revolt, for they took great care to avoid bloodshed. In other words, the plotters had just one objective in mind—to discredit the government by showing its inability to cope with disorders.

Which persons wished to discredit the government? The president singled out two groups in placing responsibility—the extreme monarchists and the anarchists.[14] Both would have profited from the fall of the provisional government. However, the monarchists had less to gain immediately from the burnings. They could simply have let the republic fall by itself under the burden of innumerable internal problems; besides, at this time the royalists were too demoralized and too disorganized to have effected a coup. On the other hand, if the government had fallen, the anarchists could have come into power with the support of great numbers of the working class, for the Socialists would have lost prestige with that sector of the population. Further evidence in support of this contention can be seen in the fact that, with the exception of Madrid, most of the burnings occurred in those areas where the social problem was most acute and where anarchist strength was centered.

If it is not known with absolute certainty who burned the churches, the irresponsibility of the government in handling the matter is fixed. The ministry had been forewarned and had refused protection. At the time, they had thought this the wisest course to avoid unpopularity with the people. But this appraisal of popular support was erroneous, for the people offered no resistance when the army was finally called out to stem the disorders. The

14. *El Sol*, May 15, 1931.

government had made a mistake and it was to prove a costly one.

In a statement issued to justify the government's inaction, Alcalá Zamora said that it had been taken by surprise and that there were too many churches and *conventos* to guard (over two hundred in Madrid alone): "If we had had the French Army, the strongest force in the world, we would not have been able to put one batallion, or even one company, at each *convento* to prevent what happened."[15] Marcelino Domingo, minister of education, said that the ministers did not know which force to use, as the civil guard had been "incapacitated" after the Sunday riots. He explained that they did not want to call out the army because this action would remind the people of the dictatorship, and it was only with hesitation that Quiepo de Llano and the troops were summoned.[16]

The material results of the burnings were, of course, the buildings burned and sacked; these numbered 107 throughout Spain. The value of the buildings destroyed in Madrid alone was estimated at five million dollars. Innumerable priceless objects were burned or stolen; relics, works of art, and whole libraries perished in the flames. For example, at the Jesuit college on Alberto Aguilera the rioters burned the archival materials of the Jesuit historian, Father Zacarías Villada, including some thirty thousand historical and paleographical notes he had been compiling since 1902 for a history of the Spanish church, and some twenty thousand volumes in the college library. In Málaga, the diocesan archives that dated back to the *reconquista* were burned.[17]

The less tangible, but much more important result of

15. *Ibid.*, May 15, 1931.
16. Marcelino Domingo, *La experiencia del poder* (Madrid, 1934), pp. 88-89.
17. Arrarás Iribarren, *Segunda república española*, p. 81 ff.

the burnings was the effect upon the church-state relationship. The government had been discredited in the eyes of the church. It began losing the support of those Catholic republicans who had sought security for their religion. The whole affair was a blot upon the hitherto untarnished republic. The monarchists, clergy and laity, now had solid evidence of the insecurity and disorder within republican Spain, something they could always appeal to. As Ramos-Oliviera cynically notes: "If the republicans, were convinced that all the conventos in Spain were not worth the life of a single republican, the clergy were no less persuaded that the overthrow of the republic was well worth the sacrifice of a few hundred chapels [sic]."[18]

The bitter smoke of burning statues was but a presage of the acrid odor of gunsmoke that would fill the air over Spain six years later.

18. *Politics, Economics and Men,* p. 440.

CHAPTER 8

THE AFTERMATH OF THE BURNINGS AND THE JUNE ELECTIONS

i

The May church burnings placed relations between the republic and the church in an entirely new light. Positions became more clearly delineated. The government by its inaction had declared its anticlericalism—it was now a truly Spanish liberal regime. There was no more talk of getting along with the church. The Holy See, however, still was not anxious to antagonize the government and it issued no formal protest against the burnings. Emboldened by the Holy See's conciliatory policy, the government began to move against the church.

The Bishop of Vitoria was ordered to leave the country because, according to the minister of justice, he had refused to stop making diocesan visits of a "marked political character."[1] De los Ríos further stated that Múgica, unlike the other bishops, was a threat to the republic.

1. *El Sol,* May 19, 1931.

Monsignor Justo de Echeguren, Vicar-General of Vitoria, protested the expulsion and claimed that the bishop had not been counseling rebellion; furthermore, no government had the right to tell a bishop to abstain from visiting his diocese.[2] The government was adamant, and Múgica settled into exile at Notre Dame de Anglet in France.

The government forbade the traditional Corpus Christi procession to be held in public that June. This was the first in a long series of banned public displays of religion. The government proclaimed the ban in the interests of security—it did not want large groups of militant Catholics congregating in public, especially in scenes charged with emotional overtones. However, in the long run, the government probably lost more support than it gained in the way of security, for processions were not so much a Catholic tradition as a Spanish one. Many Spaniards did not understand "reasons of security." To them, the fact was simply that of an anti-Catholic government persecuting their religion.

Tighter restrictions were placed on church property. A committee was appointed by the government to "guard artistic treasures in danger of being lost or stolen"—meaning religious objects of art.[3] The first step toward confiscation was taken by the minister of justice's order for a preliminary inventory of church property.

Another blow was struck at religious education. On May 21, the minister of education decreed that all private school teachers, as well as public school teachers, had to obtain university degrees in order to teach.[4] As the church's schools were mainly staffed by nuns and brothers who did not have formal university training, this action

2. *Boletín . . . Vitoria,* June 1, 1931, pp. 357-64.
3. Soto de Gongoiti, *La iglesia católica y el estado español,* pp. 150-51.
4. *Ibid.,* p. 133.

threatened to disrupt the church's educational system. However, this decree, like many others, was never fully implemented.

The most controversial step was the decree of May 22, proclaiming complete religious freedom and the termination of all civil functions by the church. Explaining the decree, De los Ríos declared that the government had no intention of harming the Catholic faith, for it was deserving of the country's respect; but by the same token, so were all religions. He noted that the decree was in accord with international law and reflected the identical position taken by the church in those countries where it was a minority religion. The decree stated that no person, in any relation with the state, was obliged to reveal his religion or take part in any religious ceremony. All faiths were authorized to perform their functions without any limitations, other than those imposed by public security.[5]

Why was the government indulging in a spree of anticlerical activity? For one thing, official religious toleration was long overdue in Spain. Various liberal regimes had played midwife to this stillborn child; it was time that the infant be allowed freedom to live. But an important factor was the church's attitude toward republican anticlericalism. Although individual bishops had protested, the Holy See had remained quiet. The anticlericals simply were overconfident. The church had not revolted after the burnings; the Holy See had not protested. Perhaps, the anticlericals thought, they had overestimated the church's power.

As it turned out, the last decree stirred the Vatican to action. For, all of the decrees were a violation of the 1851 concordat, which, it was apparent, was being abrogated by the government despite earlier promises that it would

5. *La Gaceta de Madrid,* May 22, 1931.

be honored. On the same day religious freedom and separation were decreed, the Holy See refused a *placet* (diplomatic acceptance) for Luis de Zulueta, the republic's
newly-appointed ambassador to the Holy See. Unofficial
Vatican sources declared that the action was taken because Zulueta was a "fallen-away Catholic and the author
of several well-known books of an atheistic nature."[6] The
government took the *non placet* as a reprisal for the May
riots and the separation decree. Furthermore, on May 29
the nuncio delivered a protest to the government (not
made public) concerning the church burnings, but he
called it "a short note of protest, very moderate, concerning the decrees of the last few days."[7]

The Holy See was changing its position. Moderate
conciliation had accomplished nothing, so it decided to
take a firmer line and begin protesting. Despite this
official line, however, it appears that the Vatican was preparing one major conciliatory effort. It was going to offer
a sacrificial lamb—or lion as it turned out—to appease the
government. Cardinal Segura was selected to be the
victim.

ii

The cardinal-primate had left Spain in the week following the burnings and had gone to Rome to consult
with the Pope. It appears that the two agreed upon no
definite policy—Segura's mood was far from conciliatory.
In early June, Segura sent a note to the government,
signed by himself in the name of the Spanish episcopate.
He listed the "outrages suffered by the Church" and protested the government's actions, counseling it to take

6. S.D. Dispatch 880, John W. Garrett, Ambassador to Italy, to
Stimson, May 29, 1931 (752.66A/4).
7. *El Debate*, May 30, 1931.

no further steps in regard to religion without first consulting the Holy See.[8]

On June 13, Segura returned to Spain by way of a small frontier pass in the Pyrenees. Border guards immediately notified the government. The cardinal drove on to Guadalajara, where he stopped at a *convento* of the Paulist priests. At 4:00 P.M. of the same day, representatives of the civil governor of Guadalajara, acting on orders from Madrid, placed Segura under house arrest in the *convento*. He stayed there for two days under guard. On June 15, the cardinal was handed a note from Alcalá Zamora, ordering him to leave Spain. The note said, in part: "We hoped your absence would have been prolonged, as you were counseling unrest to the public, already badly disturbed. Danger to the public spirit was seen in the terms of your violent pastoral and in your unexpected return. I hope you will stay out of Spain as long as possible."[9]

Segura said he was too ill to travel, and the *convento's* doctor agreed with him. Two other doctors were called in and they said that he was well enough to travel by automobile. At 4:30 that afternoon Segura was escorted to an automobile, driven to the frontier town of Irún, and expelled from Spain.

Before leaving, the primate gave a note to the civil governor protesting the action. The expulsion, he said, was not warranted for any reason, even not considering the fact that he was Spain's ranking churchman. He declared he had been treated as a common criminal.[10]

Alcalá Zamora answered Segura's note in a public letter. He said it was not his, but the government's, choice to expel the primate (how revealing of Alcalá Zamora's

8. *Boletín . . . Toledo,* June 8, 1931, pp. 161-62.
9. *A.B.C.,* June 19, 1931.
10. *Ibid.,* June 18, 1931.

rationalizations!); they had wanted him out of the way so that negotiations with the Holy See could be carried out in serenity. Segura, he said, had been belligerent to all the government's representatives, even to the civil governor of Toledo (José Semprún y Gurrea), a good Catholic appointed out of consideration for the cardinal. The president asserted that everything had been done for the betterment of church-state relations, and he intended no reflections on the primate's spiritual character. When a solution was worked out, he hoped Segura could return.[11]

The Holy See protested the action against the primate. *L'Osservatore Romano* said that there was no reason for the expulsion: Segura had a passport and the government had not specifically told him to stay out of the country.[12] The nuncio also protested. However, there appeared a certain undefinable lukewarmness in his protest.

In all probability—and this is conjecture—the Vatican and the nuncio were as happy to have Segura expelled as was the government. For, church-state relations would be improved with the intransigent primate out of the way. Segura had been in a powerful position—too powerful for a person not adhering to the Holy See's moderate views. How much better then, to have him in Rome, where he could be watched and kept safely out of the way. Furthermore, the Holy See had Segura to use should it wish to protest the government's religious policies in the future. The primate would be a living martyr to the church's cause. Whenever relations were to become frustrated and untenable, Segura's case would be hauled out again, and the martyr would be praised. Whenever the Holy See wanted concessions, the cardinal would be kept out of

11. *Ibid*, June 19, 1931.
12. June 17, 1931.

sight. This interpretation helps to explain much of the nature of the relationship between the republic and the Holy See.[13]

iii

During the latter part of June, the nation's attention focused upon elections for a Constituent Cortes. Although this was an important election, for the victors were to frame a constitution, the campaign was apathetic. The monarchists were disorganized and fearful—especially of having their press suspended—and popular support was overwhelmingly in favor of the government. That the Republican-Socialist coalition would elect a majority in the new Cortes was a foregone conclusion. The only real question concerned the nature of the new constitution: was it to be a radical document, as the Socialists wished, or would Spain's problems best be solved by temperate legislation, as favored by the republicans? On the religious question there was little disagreement. Anticlericalism was proving to be the unifying bond of the Republican-Socialists. The party leaders generally agreed that fairly harsh legislation was needed, specifically separation of church and state, regulation of the religious orders, including a prohibition of their teaching, and probably the confiscation of church property.

The members of Alcalá Zamora's Right Republicans were the exception within the governing coalition. The president declared that he wanted the church out of politics, but he maintained that the church's rights must be defended. Maura was the most perceptive of the republicans for he immediately saw the root of the problem: "Let us not disillusion ourselves. In Spain, for a long time

13. Iturralde, *El catolicismo*, p. 349, and Ramos-Oliviera, *Politics, Economics and Men*, p. 439, agree that the nuncio and the Holy See conspired with the government in Segura's expulsion.

we will be able to govern without the [support of] Catholics, but we will not be able to govern by attacking them."[14]

The provisional government had decreed a new electoral law of proportional representation, giving a decided advantage to coalition candidates; it had done this not only because the strength of the Republican-Socialists lay in their cohesiveness—the political Spaniard is a notorious individualist—but also to ensure minority representation. The Republican-Socialists formed a coalition including all of the leftist parties except the anarcho-syndicalists, who still remained outside of the realm of legitimate political action.

The right was not as fortunate, for it was demoralized and divided. There were monarchists, Traditionalists, Basque Nationalists, and Agrarians, all unable to unite on a coalition slate. A new party had appeared, however, calling for unity. This party was the progenitor of all moderate Catholic political groups; its formation and development are of primary importance to this study.

There had been a division between moderate and extreme Catholics long before the republic came into being. The partisans of *El Debate* and those of *El Siglo Futuro* represented these factions. Immediately after the proclamation of the republic, this division became exacerbated by the question of support for the republic.

This question split the rightists for the next five years. The moderates' position called for acceptance of the republic—not necessarily complete support, but at least not conspiracy against it. They were willing to accept the *status quo;* they were opportunists. As Catholics, their stand was supported by a half century of papal teach-

14. See *El Debate,* June 23, 1931, for Alcalá Zamora's speech; and June 16, 1931, for Maura's.

ing. Pope Leo XIII had formulated his teachings on the basis of his relations with the Third French Republic, namely that a government once established, no matter what its form, is legitimate, and no Catholic can licitly revolt against it, even if it abuses its power, for fear that the revolt may lead to greater evils. The pontiff had drawn a careful distinction between forms of government —which were always legitimate—and the government itself, which, dominated by a particular party, might be antireligious. His solution, then, was to work against the party in power by legitimate means, but never to revolt against it. This teaching had been re-emphasized by Leo's successors, and Pius XI himself had proposed it to Mexican Catholics in 1926 for their struggle against the civil power.

The Catholic extremists, on the other hand, while not denying the applicability of papal teaching, asked embarrassing questions. Was the republic a legally constituted power? Had it come into being by legitimate means? Being partisans of the monarchy, their answer was a resounding "no" to both questions. Their aim was to seek the return of the monarchy—legitimately if possible, by force if necessary.

Both groups were rationalizing their positions. Underlying the whole question was a fundamental divergency on approaches to the social question and the religious problem. The moderates wanted social ameliorization for the lower classes; the extremists wanted economic preponderance for themselves. The moderates felt that the church's interests were more important than anything else; the extremists agreed but felt that the church could function well only under a monarchy. And not the least interesting aspect of the problem was the Holy See's *volte face* on Leo XIII's position, when in 1936 it tacitly supported the Nationalist revolt.

On April 15, the moderates had taken their position. *El Debate* stated its adhesion to the republic and urged all Catholics to work for the success of the new government. The paper declared that the Holy See supported this position, which was carefully defined—with no illusions about the anticlericalism of the government leaders—but the most important point was that it considered the republic to be the legitimate Spanish government. *El Debate* further stated that moderate Catholics would use no illegal means to force the government to respect the church. It called for a "union of antirevolutionaries" to aid the common cause of religion and noted that it did not urge a return to the monarchy, for the republic was already established, and social order for the common good was more important.[15]

Both anticlericals and Catholic extremists attacked the moderates. The former warned of treachery; the moderate Catholics, they said, were simply opportunists who were trying to get in the good graces of the government (what a narrow concept of government!). *El Liberal* opined: "Let us not fool ourselves into thinking that clericalism can help in strengthening the Republic . . . this has not happened in any country."[16]

The Traditionalists, having condemned the republic before it had actually been proclaimed,[17] now turned to attacking the moderate Catholics. They repeated their political theme of "God, country, and *fueros* (rights)" within a Catholic Traditionalist monarchy, and, in a

15. Editorials of April 15, 16, and 21, 1931.
16. April 24, 1931.
17. On April 14, *El Siglo Futuro* stated that Catholic Traditionalists "will serve no liberal regime, liberal monarchy, republic, or what have you. . . . We are fundamentally antiliberal."

broadside aimed at the moderates, haughtily observed that "there is [no] method of dealing with the religious question other than by the Church's teachings."[18] Clearly, this last statement pointed to the fundamental difference in interpretation of the church's teachings.

The struggle over the religious question revolved around the enigmatic personality of Ángel Herrera Oria, editor of *El Debate.* A trim-looking forty-five, Herrera Oria was well aware of the evils of the social problem and the resultant decadence of the Spanish church. He was Tedeschini's close friend and had strong ties with the Vatican; he was a key figure in Acción Católica and the head of Acción Católica Nacional de Propagandistas, an organization of Catholic publishers.

In 1921, Herrera Oria had tried to alleviate the social problem and prevent the dechristianization of the country by proposing a plan to collect funds from the wealthier Catholics to combat social evils. All of the bishops and Pope Benedict XV lent their support, but the king refused a donation, and the plan fell through. From that moment Herrera Oria became an implacable foe of the monarch (although not of the monarchy).[19] Hence *El Debate*'s moderate position.

After the republic was proclaimed, both the left and extreme right disliked Herrera Oria because he put his religion before politics. The republicans disliked him for his support of the monarchy before the election and for his obvious opportunism now. The Traditionalists were furious with him for not adhering to their stand. Thus the division among Catholics became wider as positions were consolidated on the question of support of the republic.

The moderate Catholics were determined to battle for

18. *Ibid.,* April 15 and 16, 1931.
19. Iturralde, *El catolicismo,* pp. 344-45.

the church's rights within the legal framework of the republic. They had to form a political party. Herrera Oria proposed the idea of a political organization that would have as its aim the protection of the church's rights regardless of the form of government. Obviously, its theme and structure were to be based on those of Acción Católica. Its mission was to "look for the glory of God in all forms of government . . . [because] as citizens, we have the grave obligation to intervene for the political and social salvation of Spain." On April 29 the organization was given a name—Acción Nacional. As defined by Herrera Oria, it was "not a political party; it is an organization of social defense which will work from within the established *de facto* government in Spain to defend institutions and principles [which do not depend] essentially on any one form of government, but [which] are fundamental and basic to any society which does not wish to turn its back on twenty centuries of Christian civilization."[20]

The new organization's slogan was the defense of "religion, country, order, family, labor and property." There was no mention of form of government. The partisans of Acción Nacional wanted to make their platform so broad that it would attract all Spaniards of the right, monarchist as well as republican. And, *El Siglo Futuro* supported it at first, noting that since Acción Nacional was not a political party, Traditionalists should have no qualms about uniting behind it.[21] However, after the church burnings, the Traditionalists pulled out of the organization, for they no longer believed in any policy other than complete opposition to the republic.

20. Santiago Galindo Herrero, *Los partidos monárquicos bajo la segunda república* (Madrid, 1956), pp. 31, 52.
21. May 5, 1931.

By election time, the pro-church forces were even more widely divided. Although the episcopate issued a collective pastoral reminding Catholics of their obligation to vote for those who would "guarantee the rights of religion,"[22] the bishops realized that a fight against the Republican-Socialist coalition was hopeless.

Acción Nacional made an effort, nonetheless. Rallies were held all over Spain, and tens of thousands attended. At Pamplona, a rally was the occasion for a riot when a train carrying Catholics was attacked by extreme leftists, resulting in a battle in which one person was killed and sixty wounded. A rally was scheduled in Madrid for June 23, but the government suspended it fearing that a Catholic meeting in the center of Socialist Madrid would provoke violence. Fearing further restriction, and especially press suspension, Acción Nacional and the other rightist organization gave up actively campaigning.

Acción Nacional put 39 candidates in the running for the 475 Cortes seats (the Republican-Socialist coalition entered 507 candidates). Well-known, titled monarchists ran on its ticket, and Herrera Oria ran for one of the Madrid seats. But, defeat was a foregone conclusion.

On June 28 the nation elected a Constituent Cortes. The Republican-Socialist coalition won 386 seats; Acción Nacional won 2 (Herrera Oria lost his bid); other Catholic rightists won 44 seats. It was clear that the church was going to face a formidable struggle to prevent an anticlerical, or possibly even an antireligious, constitution from being enacted.

22. *El Debate*, June 12, 1931.

CHAPTER 9

THE CONSTITUENT CORTES
AND THE CHURCH

i

The Constituent Cortes that met in Madrid in July, 1931, was a predominantly anticlerical body. In fact, anticlericalism was the only policy that all deputies of the majority coalition had in common. The bond of anticlericalism was not a new political tactic in Europe, for continental European republican parties had long used it—the history of the Third French Republic is replete with examples—but nowhere was a bond so necessary as in the Spain of 1931. The Spanish political parties did not have deep doctrinal roots; most had been organized only a few months earlier with the primary purpose of overthrowing the monarchy. With the exception of the Socialists, few had devoted much time to party organization, or constructive legislative planning. How easy it was, then, to use anticlericalism as a binding issue to maintain republican cohesion.

Although the Republican-Socialist coalition had been formed solely to win the election, it maintained enough solidarity to see most of its campaign promises enacted into a constitution. At the same time, however, the component parties within the coalition were beginning to manifest their independence and the fatal disease of modern Spain reappeared with the trappings of political liberty; separatism was rampant.

A number of parties were represented in the Constituent Cortes. The majority coalition, completely anticlerical, was composed of 117 Socialists, 93 Radicals, 59 Radical Socialists, 27 Left Republicans, 27 Right Republicans, 32 members of the Esquerra (the Catalan Left), and 16 Galician Autonomists. Of the minority parties on the right, the two largest were the Agrarians with 26 and the Basque-Navarrese delegation numbering 14. The remainder of the deputies were scattered among federalists, monarchists, and various groups of independents.

Just as anticlericalism was the cement of the majority coalition, the minority parties used the defense of the church as their bond. The most vocal opponents of anticlericalism were the deputies from Vasconia and Navarre.

The Basques and the Navarrese, although united against anticlericalism, were strange bedfellows. The Navarre Catholics were militant Carlists but they were opposed to regional autonomy, for separatism was only a defensive tactic of Carlism. In 1931, with the anticlerical enemy at hand, they were centralists. The Basques, who had Carlist backgrounds, were separatists because they were closer to liberalism; there were large cities in Vasconia and none in Navarre. They had embraced regional autonomy as a defensive tactic, and it had become an integral part of their Carlism. The Basques, furthermore, had their own language and customs—"nationalism" as they conceived it—and after the church burnings had been impelled toward seeking a separate accord with the Holy See (which the Vatican never seriously considered); they did not want people of "baser spirit" endangering their relations with Rome.[1] The Basques had founded a strong Nationalist party under the leadership of José Antonio de Aguirre. Thus, despite the Carlism of both Basque Nationalists and Navarrese, one difference was clearly apparent—the Navarrese were determined to fight for the return of the monarchy, while the Basques wanted regional autonomy more than anything else and would compromise with any regime—as they later did—to secure these concessions.

This then, was the party structure of the Constituent Cortes; however, in such a nation of individualists, it did not take long for political ideas to become incarnate. On the religious question, two individuals became the protagonists—Manuel Azaña and José María Gil Robles. Both were entirely unprepossessing in appearance—indeed, two uglier men in all of Spain could not be found—but both men were excellent parliamentarians and were gifted with superb political ability. They were opponents on virtually every issue, but both were republicans—one by nature, the other by convenience.

Manuel Azaña Díaz, leader of the Left Republicans and minister of the army in the provisional government, was a fifty-one-year-old writer, the recently elected president of the Ateneo, Spain's literary society. Before 1931, he had held a bureaucratic position in the government, but he had devoted his main efforts to writing a number of semipolitical works, translations, and an autobiographical novel. Azaña was a born republican—and probably the

1. Domingo de Arrese, *El país vasco y los constituyentes de la segunda república* (Madrid, 1932), pp. 3-17; see also, José Antonio de Aguirre, *Entre la libertad y la revolución, 1930-1935* (Bilbao, 1935).

most forceful person in the republican ranks—but he was not a leader. His character was entirely dispassionate, and he was given over to analysis; he was an artist, not a man of action. He had already made great mistakes and errors of judgment in his reform of the army, and he was to make many more before he recognized the true dangers besetting the republic. However, if one man could be said to personify the republic—with its faults as well as virtues—that man was Azaña.

Azaña was completely anticlerical; his religious philosophy was eighteenth-century rationalism. Like most of his anticlerical colleagues, he had been educated in church schools—by the Augustinians at El Escorial—and had developed a strong antipathy toward the church. He particularly felt that if religious education could be eliminated, the future of a progressive Spain would be secure. In his desire to end the church's hold on education he had wisely seen the chink in the church's armor. However, with his time taken up with other problems, especially when he later became prime minister, he could not effectively bring his religious program to fruition.

If few persons had heard of Azaña before 1930, his antagonist was even less well known. José María Gil Robles y Quiñones was thirty-five years old, one of the youngest men in the Cortes. He was from Salamanca, where his father was a professor of law at the university. Following in the latter's footsteps, he took a law degree, winning high honors. After completing his studies he went to Madrid and became an associate editor of *El Debate*. There he came under the influence of Herrera Oria. In 1923, he, Herrera Oria and Ángel Ossorio y Gallardo had tried to form a Christian Democratic party, but royal opposition had proved too strong, and the three retreated to nurse their grievances. In the 1931 elections, Gil Robles had won election as an Agrarian from Salamanca.

Like Herrera Oria, he was an opportunist. He became a republican out of convenience, for his main concern was defending the church. He was a "social Catholic"—that is, he wanted the spirit of papal social teaching to prevail in Spain. Gil Robles' main handicap was his unwillingness to declare his republicanism until it was too late. While this gained him the political and financial support of the monarchists, it disclaimed all of his later pronouncements that he believed in the republican form of government.

ii

When the Cortes met, it elected Julián Besteiro as its president. The selection of Besteiro, a moderate Socialist and a distinguished professor of logic at the University of Madrid, was a good example of Socialist party policy. Although the Socialists were the most powerful party in the Cortes (in terms of unity and organization) they did not want positions of complete power for two reasons. First, they did not want to alarm the rightists, who generally equated Spanish socialism with bolshevism; second, if the government made any mistakes, which it surely would, the Socialists would not be held responsible. Besteiro's selection violated neither of these canons, for he was a moderate, and the post he occupied was largely powerless.

The provisional government had already foreseen that the task of drafting a constitution would be time-consuming; early in May, it had appointed a learned group under Ossorio y Gallardo to write a preliminary draft. This group, the Comisión Jurídica Asesora, presented its work, the *anteproyecto*, to the Cortes in July. As the

Comisión was predominantly conservative, the *antepro-yecto* reflected that bent, and the leftists characterized the document as merely a rewording of the 1876 constitution.

The *anteproyecto* dealt mildly with the church. It was mainly concerned with establishing the principle of religious freedom. Liberty of conscience and no official declaration of religious belief were its main tenets. Marriage and education were to be controlled by the state; any student had the right to religious education in state schools, but no teacher was obliged to teach anything against the dictates of his own conscience. The most interesting feature of the *anteproyecto*, however, was its definition of the civil status of the church, which was to be considered as a "corporation of public law."[2]

As the Comisión understood it, the idea of a corporation of public law meant that the church would be recognized as an entity within the state, but the state would reserve the right of supreme control over it. In effect, this meant that the church would be maintained in a position of privilege, while at the same time, the state would control those privileges. In principle, the Holy See could not accept this position; in practice it might, and did in other countries, where the controlling political faction was favorable to the church, or where the church had a strong political party to protect its interests. The status of the church as a corporation of public law had worked in Germany under the Weimar Republic. But in Germany the Catholic Centre party was strong enough to protect the church. In the Spain of 1931, the church could not accept this status, for it had no strong political party to protect it.

2. For the *anteproyecto*, the *proyecto*, and the constitution, see Luís Jiménez de Asúa, *Proceso histórico de la constitución de la república española* (Madrid, 1932).

Therefore, the church rejected the *anteproyecto*, and the episcopate protested with a collective pastoral. The bishops condemned it by citing its variance with the *Syllabus of Errors*, and Catholic deputies in the Cortes were warned of "their grave obligation to protect the church." The prelates counseled the faithful to organize and fight "unceasingly and prudently" for their "homes and altars" with their most powerful weapons, prayer and penitence.[3]

The majority coalition deputies also rejected the *anteproyecto*. They found it much too mild on nonreligious as well as religious questions. The document did not begin to provide the basis of the regime they wanted. Certainly, in regard to the religious problem, they wanted no laws that would recognize the Catholic church as being different from any other institution; furthermore, the *anteproyecto* did nothing to correct the abuses of religious education.

The Cortes appointed a committee to draft a new document. This committee was under the chairmanship of Luís Jiménez de Asúa, a Socialist and professor of law at the University of Madrid. Under the circumstances, with a mandate from the radical majority in the Cortes, the committee's finished document, the *proyecto parlementario*, more accurately reflected the anticlericalism of the Cortes.

The church was dealt with more harshly. It was to have no civil status different from any other institution. Marriage and education were to be under the complete control of the state, although the church could maintain its own schools, subject to state inspection. Education in the state schools was to be laical. The most stringent provisions dealt with the church's finances and the religious

3. *A.B.C.*, August 18 and 19, 1931.

orders: state-paid clerical salaries were to be abolished and the religious orders were to be dissolved and their property nationalized. Furthermore, an ambiguous provision provided that "the artistic and historical wealth of the nation is under the care of the State, which can decree [prohibitions] concerning it; . . . [and] all the national wealth . . . is subordinated to the national economic interests."

Nationalization of the property of the religious orders and the implied power to nationalize all church property followed a time-honored tradition in Spain. They were considered not so much a method of decreasing the strength of the church, as they were of solving the economic difficulties of the state. It is important to remember that Spain was suffering from the effects of the worldwide economic depression. Financial instability had been one factor causing the fall of the dictatorship, and the republicans themselves were maintaining the stability of the *peseta* only with difficulty. Confiscation of church property would go a long way toward solving the government's economic problems.

The church was not willing to let these proposals go uncondemned, but to avoid antagonism the episcopate did not directly protest. Instead, it relied on the laity, who began to flood the Cortes with protests, petitions, telegrams, letters, and phone calls. All urged the rejection of the *proyecto* and many complained about the government's anticlerical policies.

For, in the meantime, the government had been moving against the church. On July 9 it had decreed the secularization of cemeteries. Previously, the church could refuse burial to non-Catholics in the state-maintained cemeteries (which belonged to the church); these deceased then had to be buried in private cemeteries. The decree of July 9 made it mandatory that anyone desiring a religious funeral had to state so in his will; if not stated, his survivors could decide the matter.[4] While few Catholics could complain about the letter of this decree, in practice many anticlerical municipal governments ignored the decision of survivors; given the high degree of illiteracy and the fact that few Spaniards bothered with wills, many Catholics were denied religious funerals. These actions caused a storm of protest. So also did the changing of street names: for example, the Bishop of Ávila objected to renaming the Plaza de Santa Teresa the Plaza de la República.[5]

Not a few of the anticlerical intellectuals protested the government's actions. Unamuno became a critic of separation, observing that the republic had nothing to gain by antagonizing the church, especially since the clergy had, in the main, proved submissive to the government.[6] Gregorio Marañón warned that if the *proyecto* were enacted as a constitution, a spiritual civil war would result.[7]

These wiser counsels did not prevail in the Cortes debates that followed.

iii

In the middle of August, while committees were struggling with the *proyecto*, while militant Catholics were protesting to the Cortes, and while wiser Spaniards simply tried to maintain a position of balance, the Segura affair came to a climax.

Although the cardinal had been expelled, he was still primate of Spain, and from across the border in France

4. Soto de Gongoiti, *La iglesia católica y el estado español*, p. 118.
5. *El Debate*, August 14, 1931.
6. *The New York Times Magazine*, May 24, 1931.
7. *El Sol*, October 8, 1931.

he had continued to protest the government's actions. In July he had written the president, citing papal teaching and the 1851 concordat to point out the government's errors, and he asked to be allowed to return to Spain "for the common good," adding that he was willing to forgive his enemies. In that same month, he had directed two pastoral letters to Spanish Catholics, counseling them to obey the civil power when not contrary to the laws of God and the church.[8] At the same time, a number of clerical visitors crossed the frontier daily to see the primate. On August 14, the government decided to take action.

On that day, the Vicar-General of Vitoria was arrested and searched by the border guards at San Sebastián. They claimed that he was carrying documents from Segura to the bishops, instructing them to sell all the church property they could and send the money out of the country, for the primate feared that church property would soon be confiscated—a not unreasonable fear, considering the tenor of the *proyecto*. Segura denied this, claiming that he had only told the bishops to fight, by legal means, attempts to confiscate certain "reserve funds" of the dioceses.[9]

Whatever the facts, the government was alarmed. Too much capital had already fled the country in April when many of the wealthy Spaniards had left. Therefore, the nuncio was informed of the government's displeasure and was asked if the Holy See had any knowledge of Segura's activities. Tedeschini, of course, denied Vatican complicity.

8. *Boletín . . . Toledo*, July 8, 1931, pp. 221-29; July 23, 1931, p. 237; August 2, 1931, pp. 225-26.

9. *El Sol*, August 15, 1931; Iturralde, *El catolicismo*, pp. 339-40; and Jesús Requejo San Román, *El Cardenal Segura* (Madrid, n.d.), pp. 194-203.

The government wanted to end the Segura affair completely, but it could not act immediately for there was a threat of insurrection within the country. The Basques had never accepted the expulsion of Bishop Múgica (the Basque delegation had petitioned the Cortes to allow him to return), and feeling had already been running high against the anticlerical *proyecto*. The detention and searching of the Basques' vicar-general raised agitation to such a pitch that the government was forced to send in troops and suspend the Basque Catholic press to forestall violence.

Having enforced these security measures, the government took further action. First, it reiterated its decree of May 2 prohibiting the sale or transferal of church property. Then, on August 22, it ordered that Segura and Múgica be removed from their sees and stripped of their episcopal rank.[10]

Consultations with the nuncio followed, for this action brought the government directly into conflict with the Holy See. The government did not have the legal right to dismiss the two bishops (the abrogated concordat established the norms for appointment but said nothing about dismissal), and not even the Pope could deprive the prelates of their episcopal powers.

Now that the nuncio and the provisional government were brought together again, offers and counteroffers were considered. The government wanted the Segura affair closed for good; the demands of domestic tranquillity could ill afford any more incidents with the exiled primate. The Holy See was willing to sacrifice Segura, but it wanted assurances that the *proyecto* would be rejected in favor of more moderate religious legislation.

Alcalá Zamora, Maura, and Lerroux could give no as-

10. *El Debate*, August 23, 1931.

surances other than that they would try to do what they could. After all, with the Cortes in session, their own political life depended upon the whim of the deputies. They could make no promises. It was up to the Holy See to do what it could to placate the Cortes.

On the eve of the opening Cortes debates on the *proyecto* in early September, Francisco Cardinal Vidal y Barraquer, the Archbishop of Tarragona (Catalonia), having recently returned from Rome, indicated the Holy See's mood. He declared that the clergy would be willing to support the government on all temporal matters "provided the dignity of the church be retained."[11]

The Holy See's final offer came a week before the Cortes began debating the religious question. On October 1, it announced that Cardinal Segura had resigned both the Primacy of Spain and the See of Toledo. He would be temporarily replaced by a vicar *pro tem*, but the See of Toledo was declared officially vacant.[12] This event had implications.

First, the unwilling victim was sacrificed in the hope that the *proyecto* would not become the constitution.[13] Then, the fact that the Holy See did not immediately name a successor to the primacy was intended as a sign

11. *A.B.C.*, September 1, 1931.
12. *Ibid.*, October 1, 1931.
13. Iturralde, *El catolicismo*, pp. 347-49, says that the Pope sent Monsignor Maglione, the nuncio in Paris, to Segura to ask him to resign the primacy. Segura demanded the request in writing, eventually consented, and sent his resignation to the Pope, stating that he did so not of his own free will. As a postscript, he included his resignation from the College of Cardinals! When Pius received this, he called Segura to Rome, treated him kindly, and got him to retract his resignation as cardinal. He asked him to modify his resignation of the primacy by stating that he did so freely. Segura refused, saying that it was against his conscience: "I have told Your Holiness that your wishes are always my orders, but to do this I would have to lie, and this I cannot do." Finally, however, the cardinal gave in and resigned, and settled down in Rome.

of disapproval of the government's policies. However, the government was elated and De los Ríos proudly noted that this was only the third time in modern history that a primacy had been resigned: "Not even Philip II succeeded in removing a primate."[14]

Would the Cortes accept the Holy See's offer? Would a policy of moderation prevail? There were warnings of unfavorable consequences: Maura threatened to resign if the *proyecto* became law. The anticlericals could shrug off this threat, for they could do without Maura. But, the anticlericals did not realize that his views were shared by millions of Catholics, and no Spanish government could afford to do without them.

iv

"Spain is no longer Catholic."[15] With these words, Manuel Azaña began a speech marking the culmination of the debate on the religious question. It was the early evening of Tuesday, October 13, and the Cortes had heard four days of acrimonious charges hurled back and forth in the most heated discussion since the debates began.

Many arguments had been presented in those emotion-laden days, and the speeches had ranged from the classically precise anticlericalisms of De los Ríos, through Gil Robles' elaborately Thomistic defense of the church, to the unintelligible rationalizations of Alcalá Zamora. There were also the vulgarities and superficialities of the lesser anticlericals.

Briefly, the anticlerical argument presented by the minister of justice made three points. First, clerical stipends would have to be abolished, for they were payment

14. *A.B.C.*, October 1, 1931.
15. *Diario de sesiones de las cortes constituyentes de la república española* (Madrid, 1931-33), October 13, 1931, p. 1666. Hereafter cited as *DSCC*.

for services rendered; separation would end these services and the payment for them. Second, any accord with the Holy See could not be negotiated until the Cortes had legislated the church's position. Finally, the religious orders would have to be the subject of special legislation and would probably face nationalization of their property and restrictions on their teaching activities.[16]

Most of the anticlericals wanted special legislation against the Jesuits—dissolution of the order and nationalization of its property. The pretense for this action was to be that the fourth vow of special obedience to the Pope (which many but not all Jesuits take) constituted an oath of allegiance to a foreign power.

Some of the anticlericals turned to arguing in obvious bad taste, with sly innuendos concerning clerical celibacy and coarse attacks on the religious orders. A few felt that monks and nuns were kept in *conventos* against their wills and wanted a complete dissolution of all orders. Eduardo Barriobero, Federalist, exhibited probably the nadir of anticlerical thought with his opinion that monks could not claim legal equality in the same way that insane people could not. Monks, he said, were demented anyway, for they sacrificed all the pleasures of life; the problems of the material order were enough to occupy anyone without their having to think of the spiritual life.[17]

Could Catholics hope for reason and moderation when speeches like this were wildly cheered?

The Catholic argument, as presented by Gil Robles, was, briefly, that church and state were two entities, each with particular aims which in theory should not conflict with each other. Catholics were willing to admit separation as long as the rightful and just aims of both were

16. *DSCC,* October 8, 1931, pp. 1528-34.
17. *DSCC,* October 10, 1931, pp. 1586-92.

recognized; church and state should complement, not replace, each other. Concerning the religious orders, he declared that the proposal to limit them and nationalize their property was a negation of the spirit of the constitution and violated the principles of individual liberty, freedom of association, and legal equality, integral elements already voted into the constitution.[18]

Gil Robles' argument was bolstered by warnings from other Catholic deputies that the republic would be seriously endangered and weakened if the Cortes legislated harshly against the church. All pointed out that the church was the bulwark of the rights of man and of liberty, despite those individual Catholics who profaned the church's teachings; and furthermore, the deputies should distinguish between the church and those politico-religious groups that were not truly representative of it.

True to his agreement with the nuncio, Alcalá Zamora spoke to the Cortes in an attempt to soften the measures against the church. Lerroux did not honor his word, perhaps because he believed that nothing could be done; but probably because he did not want to commit himself. He claimed pressing business at Geneva and departed for a League of Nations meeting.

Alcalá Zamora declared that the *proyecto* was not motivated by liberty and justice, but by religious prejudice. Completely evading the real question and obfuscating the idea of democracy, he stated: "The real problem is: are the Catholics in Spain a majority or a minority? . . . if they are a majority, and if Spain is a true democracy, one cannot legislate against the rights of the majority. . . . If they are a minority, then their rights must be protected."

However, despite statements like this, the president

18. *DSCC*, October 8, 1931, pp. 1534-39.

did make some valid criticisms. He remarked that it would be unwise to repress the church because of its orthodoxy and intolerance, for this would "simply transfer the role of the institution from that of hangman to victim"; besides, intolerance had never been the exclusive domain of any one institution in Spain. He warned against dissolution of the religious orders, because "no order is by nature an enemy of the State"; but, if the Cortes was determined to take action against them it should be done in the form of a flexible law, not a rigid norm of the constitution. Finally, he warned that he would have to leave the government if the *proyecto* were approved.[19]

While the debate continued, the Cortes received a letter from the five provincial superiors of the Jesuits in Spain. The priests declared that they had recognized the new regime and had complied with its dictates in complete fidelity. The Jesuits, they said, were an intimate part of Spain's history, and being Spaniards, they were entitled to the same rights as other citizens. To the charges that the society was incompatible with republicanism, the superiors pointed out that Jesuits throughout the world got along with every type of government. They did not ask any favors but simply that justice be done.[20]

This was the history of those four days before Azaña rose to deliver one of the most important speeches of his life, on October 13. The Cortes had just approved Article 3 of the constitution by a vote of 267 to 41. Article 3 read, "The Spanish State does not have an official religion."

Azaña began by noting that none of the problems being discussed had been invented by the republic; the

19. *DSCC*, October 10, 1931, pp. 1602-11.

20. The document is in José de Manterola, *La disolución en España de la companía de Jesús, ante sus consecuencias, el sentido común y el derecho* (Barcelona, 1934), pp. 197-206.

deputies were simply exposing those of the monarchy (Azaña was not above rationalizing either, for these were Spanish problems, not exclusively governmental ones). The chief problem was religious: "The premise of the [religious] problem, now political, I have formulated thus: Spain is no longer Catholic." There was no reason to favor the church in any way. It was purposeless to point to the greatness of the chuch in the sixteenth century and to say that it was the republic's obligation to keep the decadent institution alive, he said, for the church was no longer the leader of the nation.

Concerning the religious orders, Azaña admitted that it was a contradiction to guarantee liberty to all on the one hand and to limit that of the monks on the other. But, the question was one of national security, for the republic and the orders could not coexist in Spain; one was bound to destroy the other. And, although it was not democratic to prohibit religious education, the "public mental health" had to be preserved, for the church, he claimed, taught everything contrary to the basis of the modern democratic state.[21]

After Azaña spoke, the session was recessed for three hours. The Cortes then reconvened at 12:10 A.M., now October 14. The anticlericals wanted to end discussion on the religious problem and force a vote. They had the majority necessary to do so, but the Catholic deputies introduced numerous moderating amendments, hoping to forestall the vote; this only dragged out the session. As the night wore on, many deputies drifted back to their hotels. The Radical Socialists walked out *en masse*, protesting that the *proyecto* was too moderate. Finally, at 6:00 A.M. the vote was taken. Of the 470 deputies, a few over half remained. The final tally was 178 to 59 in favor

21. *DSCC*, October 13, 1931, pp. 1666-72.

of the religious section of the *proyecto,* with amendments, which now became incorporated as Article 26 of the constitution. When the result was announced, a brief fist-fight broke out on the floor between some of the anti-clericals and the Vasconavarros. Finally, at 6:30 the historic session was ended.

Article 26 of the Constitution read:

All faiths will be considered as associations under a special law.

The State, the regions, the provinces, and the municipalities will not favor, maintain, nor economically aid the Churches, religious institutions, or associations.

A special law will regulate the total extinction of the clerical budget, within a maximum time of two years.

Those religious orders which [by their statutes] impose, above the three canonical vows, another one of obedience to an authority distinct from the State, are dissolved. Their property will be nationalized and used for charitable and educational purposes.

The remainder of the religious orders will be submitted to a special law, to be passed by these Constituent Cortes, based on the following norms:

1. Those whose activities constitute a danger to the State will be dissolved.
2. Those which are allowed to stay shall be registered with the Ministry of Justice.
3. They shall be forbidden to acquire or keep, either themselves or through an intermediary, more property than . . . is necessary for their living needs or for the direct completion of the distinctive goals [of the order].
4. They shall be forbidden to engage in industry, commerce, or teaching.
5. They shall be submitted to all of the tax laws of the country.
6. They shall be obliged to give an annual accounting to the State of their investments, in relation to the purposes of the order.

The property of the religious orders can be nationalized.[22]

22. Jiménez de Asúa, *La constitución,* p. 186.

By its very nature, Article 26 committed the republic to a fight against the church, for there were some provisions that violated canon law and that the church would never accept. It could live with economic separation and the dissolution of the Jesuits, as it could with some of the laws against the other religious orders. But the church would fight to the end the prohibition against the orders' teaching, for this struck at the basis of the church's educational system.

By voting its policies of the moment into a constitution, the government was legally bound to carry them out, as constitutional revision before a period of four years was forbidden. Furthermore, Article 26 established the machinery for another bitter debate by requiring this same Cortes to legislate on the religious orders. Time would show that no government could completely carry out the legislation, and while most Catholics obeyed the laws, few were convinced that the constitution had the binding power of legality.

Thus, a false issue led to a permanent breach in the nation's solidarity. The enforcement of Article 26 became a tenet of faith for the anticlericals, while at the same time Catholics felt that nothing could be accomplished until the constitution was revised. Greater issues were forgotten and greater dangers overlooked. In its moment of peril five years later, the republic could not command the allegiance of Catholics mainly because of Article 26.

There were immediate serious results. The Basque, Navarre, and Agrarian deputies walked out of the Cortes and refused to attend further debates, with the result that the remainder of the *proyecto* was passed with little debate at a pace that alarmed even its author. The other articles pertaining to the religious question established freedom of conscience, the secularization of cemeteries, a

requirement for governmental approval of public manifestations of religion (i.e., processions), state control of
marriage and divorce, implied state control of all private
property, and laic education (although religious schools
were permitted, under state inspection).

As they had warned, Alcalá Zamora and Maura resigned from the government, taking all moderating influence with them (although both still proclaimed their
adhesion to the republic). Manuel Azaña was elected
president of the provisional government, this meant a decided swing to the left.

Probably the most important immediate consequence
of the passage of Article 26 was that it gave Catholics a
rallying point, and they began agitating for constitutional
revision even before the Cortes had finished debating the
remainder of the constitution.

In sum, the passage of Article 26 was disastrous for the
republic.[23]

v

Catholics were aware of one important fact. This was
that Spaniards had never been sticklers for constitutional
implementation, per se. Seven constitutions in the past 120
years had not wedded even liberals to the principles of
strict enactment. Therefore, the execution of the religious
legislation would depend on the government; an anti-

23. Madariaga, *Spain,* p. 395, says that if the republic had chosen
to live under the 1851 concordat, it would have "inherited the unique
privileges which the Spanish State had conquered over Rome in the
course of centuries." Instead, "the bigots and priests of the Holy Anticlerical Church" were motivated by a spirit of "petty, almost vindictive
anticlericalism." Ramos-Oliviera, *Politics, Economics and Men,* p. 445,
says that Article 26 "breathed new life into a soulless Church" and that
the middle class had persuaded the proletariat that the religious problem was the most important. "The conduct of the Church and the
ignorance of the common people conspired together to create this il-
lusion in the popular mind." Brenan, *Spanish Labyrinth,* p. 237, also
agrees that Article 26 was disastrous for the republic.

clerical ministry would probably carry out the laws, while
a ministry favorable to the church would ignore them.
Hence, immediate church policy was to agitate for the
election of a new Cortes, which it hoped would be less
anticlerical. For the present the church knew that it still
could not afford to antagonize the government for fear
that the laws would be executed immediately.

Thus, the Holy See did not protest directly to the government. Instead, Cardinal Pacelli sent a telegram from
the Pope to the nuncio, declaring that the episcopate
should protest the laws and that the "harm . . . be re-
paired by just and legal means."[24] Through Pacelli, the
Pope also sent a letter to the superior general of the Jesuits, congratulating the society because a legislative assembly had recognized their special devotion to the Pope
and incidentally answering the charges of "foreign allegiance" by quoting Bismarck's words that "a power
which has the obedience of millions of citizens in a country cannot be considered foreign."[25]

Finally, the Segura affair was brought up again and
the Pope released for publication the letter he had sent
Segura when the latter had resigned the primacy. The
Pope had said in the letter: "In this action . . . we have
another . . . proof of your . . . zeal for men's souls. . . .
In the hope of contributing to the greater good . . . or
even of abolishing pretexts for inflicting greater evils . . .
you did not hesitate to sacrifice yourself. . . ."[26]

But, this was all; the nuncio delivered no formal protest. When Tedeschini, as dean of the diplomatic corps,
paid his customary visit to the new president, Azaña, on
October 16, he told reporters that Azaña was an old friend
of his and that his visit had nothing to do with the reli-

24. *A.B.C.*, October 17, 1931.
25. Manterola, *La disolución*, p. 229-30.
26. *A.B.C.*, October 20, 1931.

gious question. As for the church, he said, "it is wounded [but] not hostile."[27]

The episcopate responded mildly; they likewise were conditioned by fear that the laws would be executed immediately if the government were provoked. Most of the bishops ordered days of prayer and told their faithful to work within the realm of legality to prevent the execution of the laws and the enactment of further legislation against the church.[28]

The populace reacted more violently. Many anticlericals felt the religious laws too mild, and in Valencia a large anticlerical parade was held, calling for more stringent legislation. The anarcho-syndicalists were, of course, not satisfied at all, and a group of them set fire to a Carmelite *convento* in Santander.

The Catholic laity protested also. In Vasconia open violence was expected at any moment. In Madrid, Catholic groups deluged the nunciature with letters and telegrams pledging support. A riot was started in a Madrid theater by Catholic students protesting the showing of Pérez de Ayala's anticlerical play, *A.M.D.G.*

What was the ministry's reaction? Recall that it was not as rabidly anticlerical as the Cortes. Also, many of the statements made in the Cortes were simply for effect —to appease the voters back home or to be put on record. The ministry fully intended to implement the legislation, but at its own pace. Thus, on October 16, it decreed that the religious orders were *not* to close their schools, under pain of confiscation;[29] if the religious schools were closed immediately the majority of the nation's secondary students would overload the state schools.

The most crushing blow dealt the church in these days

27. *Ibid.*, October 16, 1931.
28. Gomá y Tomás, *Antilaicismo*, II, 189-211.
29. *A.B.C.*, October 16, 1931.

after the passage of Article 26 was the Cortes' action of continuing itself in session as a national assembly. This was a great setback for the Catholics, for they had hoped for new elections to gain control of the Cortes. Indeed, complaints and demands for constitutional revision became so vociferous that the government had to prohibit public meetings on the matter in order to maintain order.

vi

By early December, the Cortes had completed the constitution and elected Azaña as the new premier. In the selection of a president—a largely honorary position—the Cortes resurrected Alcalá Zamora from political oblivion. Few of the democratic liberals or Socialists liked Alcalá Zamora, but they felt that as president he would lend moderate respectability to the government and also his selection would tend to appease growing Catholic opposition. Alcalá Zamora gratefully accepted the office, salving his outraged conscience of October 14 by reasoning that he could do more from within than from without to lead the government to moderation.

Positions on the religious question were defined by this time. The smoke and debris of the constitutional battle had been cleared away. There was time for all to formulate more carefully-thought-out policies.

The government's aim was to remain in power until the constitution was fully implemented. The religious legislation would be executed, but with moderation; that the Jesuits had not yet been dissolved was a sign of this leniency. But there were no illusions that the religious legislation would be forgotten.

The moderate Catholics, represented by Gil Robles, Herrera Oria, and Acción Nacional, made their position clear. Herrera Oria spoke in Valencia, shortly before

Christmas, summing up their stand. He made the distinction between a constituted power (the republic) and legislation (Article 26), declaring that a constituted power always deserved support, but legislation against the law of God or the church did not require obedience; in fact, it was the Catholic's duty to resist unjust laws. He stressed that moderate Catholics intended no violence and that they were going to work within the law to achieve their aims.

The moderate Catholic leader emphasized that all rightists had to unify and forget their political differences. Only in an organization like Acción Nacional was this possible. As for the constitution, he warned, Spaniards could do only one of two things: either revise it completely and rapidly, or continue to live outside it.[30]

The episcopate also arrived at a definition of its position in a collective pastoral published on New Year's Day, 1932. The prelates repeated that it was their duty to guide the faithful. The constitution, they charged, was animated by a spirit of sectarianism, for the church had been excluded from political life, and its "rights and liberties negated." Specifically, they protested the abolition of clerical salaries; the constitutional action taken against the Jesuits and other religious orders, they said, was a violation of international law, as well as of the Spanish constitution itself.

The bishops reminded Catholics of their duty to assure their children a religious education and of their obligation to be loyal and obedient to both the Pope and the civil government. Catholics were to use all "just and legitimate means" to repair the damage done. "The

30. Ángel Herrera Oria, *La posición de la derecha española en la política actual,* discurso pronunciado . . . en el Teatro Apolo de Valencia, December 21, 1931 (Madrid, 1932).

Church," they said, "is above partisan politics . . . and Catholic teaching is not in conflict with the civil life."[31]

By the beginning of 1932 stands were taken: the government would continue its policies against the church and the Catholics would counter them by legal means. The constitution, however, was an irreparable deed. It committed the republic to a war against the church and it gave the antirepublicans and rightists a rallying point. From this time on, the entire legal basis of the republic fairly begged for civil disobedience from Catholics.

31. *A.B.C.*, January 1, 1932.

CHAPTER 10

THE LEFT IN POWER: IMPLEMENTATION OF THE RELIGIOUS LEGISLATION

From January, 1932, until the spring of 1933 the politico-religious problem was relegated to a secondary place in national affairs. The government considered the matter closed; the constitution had established the law, and the ministry's task was to execute it. The government had more important problems to face, ones it had put off until the constitution was enacted. The social problem, always acute, was becoming exacerbated by the far-reaching effects of the depression. At the same time, the separatist provinces were clamoring for autonomy.

Manuel Azaña's coalition ministry was balanced on a precarious foundation. It had to maintain an equilibrium while facing threats of a restoration from the monarchists on the one hand and the implementation of the proletarian revolution on the other. At the same time, the coalition was breaking apart. Lerroux withdrew his ninety-three Radicals and refused to participate in the government; the wily old demagogue realized that the Azaña government was bound to make mistakes and he wanted the Radicals to have no share in the blame. Thus, the Left Republicans were forced into a greater reliance upon the Socialists.

The Republican-Socialist union was based on a fiction, for the two groups were ideologically opposed. The crux of their disharmony was the nature of the republic. The republicans felt that the revolution was ended. The constitution was passed and there was no need for further legislation; the government's task, they felt, was simply to implement the constitution. The Socialists, on the other hand, felt that the revolution had just begun, and that the constitution was merely the blueprint for the future classless society. The inevitable clash between the two came on the issue of agrarian reform. The republicans wanted landed property redistributed into small individual landholdings; the Socialists wanted collective farms. In the impasse, little agrarian reform took place although an agrarian reform law was passed.

However, the two acted together in some matters. A Catalan Autonomy Statute was passed, the army was reorganized, and educational reform was begun. On one issue, the republicans and Socialists had no difficulty in maintaining unity of purpose: the religious laws were carried out to the letter.

i

Over a month had passed since the constitution had been approved. Technically, the Society of Jesus was dissolved. As yet, no decree to this effect had been issued by the government and the Jesuits meanwhile maintained their prerepublican form of existence, albeit uneasily. The government was biding its time.

On January 12, 1932, Juan Botella Asensio, Radical-Socialist, broached the matter in the Cortes, asking why the Jesuits had not yet been dissolved. Álvaro de Albornoz, the new minister of justice, replied that the ministry was waiting for the proper time, so that the decree could be carried out effectively.[1] As a matter of fact, at the time, the ministry was preoccupied with the anarcho-syndicalists who were not only fomenting industrial strikes but were also attempting open insurrection against the government.

The Jesuits heeded the warning, and the following day the Society presented a plea to the government. They protested the dissolution of the Society, noting that only one-tenth of the Jesuits took the fourth vow of obedience to the Pope and that "all Catholics are bound to obey the Pope on spiritual matters," so that on this question, "there is only an organizational difference between the Jesuits and other Catholics."[2]

There the matter rested for a few days, until events in Vasconia finally led to action by the government. These northern provinces had been seething ever since the constitutional debates, and violence finally erupted in Bilbao, where a street fight between Catholics and Socialists ended in the death of four persons. An infuriated mob then marched on the churches and succeeded in burning five of them.

The government supported the mob. It closed one *convento* and fined the superior of another 10,000 *pesetas* for having broken the peace by firing upon the mob attacking the building. The government also suspended *El*

1. *DSCC,* January 12, 1932, pp. 3109-13.
2. Manterola, *La disolución,* pp. 217-18.

Debate; the paper had criticized the ministry for encouraging anticlericalism and for ignoring its duties by making no attempt to arrest the incendiaries.[3] With this newspaper silenced, the government then proceeded to act against the Jesuits.

On January 23, the decree of dissolution was issued.[4] The Society of Jesus was dissolved on Spanish territory; the state would no longer recognize the juridical personality of the Society nor its *conventos* or schools. The members of the Society were to cease living in common by February 2, 1932, ten days after the promulgation of the decree. They were forbidden to sell any property after January 23, and within the ten-day period, all banks and other firms with Jesuit-owned stock were to submit a listing of these to the government. All Jesuit property was to be nationalized and used for educational and charitable purposes, except the church buildings, which would be turned over to the local parish on condition that no former Jesuit be employed by that parish. Finally, the decree authorized the establishment of an expropriation commission to administer the nationalization of the property and handle any claims that might arise.

The church thundered its protest, the loudest yet voiced against the government's religious policies. It had hoped that the religious laws would not be executed, but it was now faced with a *fait accompli* and thus could make its displeasure known. The nuncio delivered a note to the government in which he stated that the fourth vow was simply an "explicit, solemn ratification of the normal clerical vow of obedience" and was essentially no different from it. He charged that the government had refused to

3. Editorial of January 20, 1932.
4. Soto de Gongoiti, *La iglesia católica y el estado español*, pp. 139-42.

carry out its promise to respect the church's rights and cited the articles of the constitution violated by the dissolution.[5]

Cardinal Vidal y Barraquer, acting as spokesman for the episcopate, denounced the decree as an insult to the Pope.[6] Catholics all over Spain protested, especially in the Basque provinces. At St. Ignatius Loyola's birthplace, crowds lined up outside Jesuit *conventos* and filed through to pay their respects. Similar scenes occurred in most Spanish cities.

Discussion in the Cortes centered on the decree. Some deputies pressed for the dissolution of the other religious orders. Claims and counterclaims were made; one deputy noted that the Jesuits' mercantile activity could not be kept secret now, in view of the number of banks and industries that had closed or suspended payments since the publication of the decree (an observation not founded in fact).[7] Other deputies rose to defend the society. Pildáin, the priest deputy from Vasconia, prophesied that the Jesuits would once again return to pray over the tombs of those who had ousted them.[8] Finally, after Albornoz reviewed the government's reasons for the decree, the Cortes voted to end discussion of the matter.

Therefore, on February 2, 1932, the Society of Jesus ceased to have civil existence in Spain. For all practical purposes, the government had made a mistake. It had forgotten that it was dealing with an organization which had been expelled or dissolved four times in the previous 120 years. The Jesuits had learned from the experience but the anticlericals had forgotten. The most obvious

5. Note delivered on January 29, published in *L'Osservatore Romano*, February 8, 1932.
6. *A.B.C.*, January 27, 1932.
7. *DSCC*, January 29, 1932, pp. 3518-23.
8. *DSCC*, February 4, 1932, pp. 3610-12.

mistake the government made was dissolving the Jesuits instead of expelling them; this nullified the government's alleged intentions. Dissolution meant simply that the Society ceased to exist in the eyes of the government. Jesuits were legally no longer Jesuits or members of a religious order. Therefore, they could continue to live in Spain as private individuals and teach in private schools, while the government's most effective method of control over them—their organizational bond—was legally nonexistent.

Of the 3600 Spanish Jesuits affected by the decree, many decided to go abroad, to America, Belgium, and Holland; but many decided to stay in Spain, and were, of course, legally entitled to do so, although under the restrictions imposed by the decree. The government had alienated these Jesuits without bringing them under control. If individual Jesuits had once been republican (some were) they were no longer. If the Society once posed a threat to the republic, that threat still remained, now propertyless and disgruntled.

The mistake was compounded in the field of education. Twenty-one *colegios* (secondary schools), two universities, and four other centers of higher education were closed. Almost seven thousand students were turned out of the Jesuit schools, many to burden the already overloaded state schools. Two astronomical observatories, a leprosarium, and three seminaries sending missionaries to staff schools in India, Cuba, and the Philippines were also closed. Salvador de Madariaga, later a minister of education (in 1934) noted the result: "The Republic ... lightheartedly closed down the only type of school that, for all its imperfection, bore some slight resemblance to a secondary school—the Jesuit *colegio.*"[9]

9. Salvador de Madariaga, *Anarquía o jerarquía: Ideario para la constitución de la 3ª. república española* (Madrid, 1935), p. 248.

Then there were the financial complications. Estimates of the value of Jesuit property ranged from the absurdly low to the ridiculously high; it is impossible to tell the actual value. When the confiscations began, officials found that many of the Jesuits' buildings had been rented by the Society and thus could not be nationalized; since their return from the expulsions during the First Republic, the Jesuits had purchased little real property. Other Jesuit-used property was registered in the names of laymen; this was especially true of the Jesuit's mercantile and commercial investments.

The expropriation commission spent the next four years trying to settle these problems. It had to deal with the claims of those who had investments in the confiscated property; these investors could reclaim their money, with interest, if they could prove no affiliation with the Society. The commission was still working its way through this legal maze four years later when the Civil War began. By that time, it had realized confiscations worth some $20,000,000.[10]

In the balance, what can be said of the action against the Jesuits? In all probability, the Society was predominantly antirepublican. But, it was hardly a threat to the republic; certainly nothing compared to the army or the monarchists. Furthermore, the Society, being a church organization, was open to the influences of the moderate Catholics. In other words, in view of the very real dangers posed by extreme rightists and leftists, the government's actions against the Jesuits appear as pointless as they were dangerous.

ii

The abolition of clerical salaries was started in the spring of 1932, for Article 26 provided for the cessation

10. Ramos-Oliviera, *Politics, Economics and Men*, p. 446.

of all stipends within a two-year period. The 1931 clerical budget, established by the monarchy had been 66,000,000 *pesetas*, but the bishops' salaries had been suspended at the proclamation of the republic. Stipends for 1932 were decreased to 29,500,000 *pesetas*, and the total 1933 clerical budget was set at 5,000,000 *pesetas*. Late in 1932 the Cortes voted to end all clerical salaries by November 11, 1933.

The church was now faced with the very serious problem of supporting some 35,000 priests, 7,000 of whom were over fifty years of age. As rumors concerning the wealth of the church had been greatly exaggerated, and because the church was forbidden by law to sell any of its property, the only way it could obtain money was from the faithful. This posed a difficult problem, for the clergy had never asked Catholics for regular periodic donations. Spaniards were not in the habit of contributing to the church, and it was apparent that they would take a long time getting accustomed to the idea. For example, Cardinal Ilundáin pleaded for just one peseta ($.10) per month from each family in the Archdiocese of Seville to solve financial problems; the amount asked for was not given.[11]

The abolition of clerical salaries hurt not only the church, for many priests now found themselves with their only source of financial support gone; it was also a tactless mistake on the part of the government. Whatever the basis of the stipends—whether for services rendered or in compensation for the *desamortización*—the clergy had been treated as civil servants. The abolition of their stipends appeared as the action of an ungrateful government. The rural clergy were especially hurt; the wealthier urban clergy would hardly miss the small stipends, but the rural priests depended on governmental support. As

11. *Boletín . . . Sevilla*, February 7, 1933, pp. 29-33.

a result this group, whose support, moral and otherwise, the democratic liberals could have used, was alienated from the republic.

The government moved on to the implementation of other laws. Of these, the establishment of civil marriage and divorce was probably the least irritating to both sides. Catholics were simply reminded by their pastors that only canonical marriage was valid for them, and they were permitted to participate in the civil ceremony in order to comply with the law.

The divorce law had somewhat different connotations. Previously, a church court, the Tribunal de la Rota, had been granted supreme power to judge on cases of annulment without recourse to Rome. This power had been extended to the Spanish church by the papacy, and Spain was the only country to have this privilege. The nuncio had directed the Tribunal, which was supported by state funds. With the promulgation of the divorce law, the fiscal support of the Tribunal ceased, and the state no longer recognized its jurisdiction. Without funds, the Tribunal could no longer operate and canonical cases for annulment now had to go to Rome.

Although the church condemned the divorce law, its implementation caused little friction; after the first rush of cases, the divorce average leveled off, and of course few, if any, practicing Catholics sought recourse in the divorce courts.

iii

The government's plans to do away with religious education posed the most serious threat to the church and also brought the ministry face to face with a larger problem—that of providing a replacement for the church-operated schools. In 1931, there were some 400,000 students in the church schools, while at least half a million children were receiving no education at all.[12] Therefore, to comply with the law, the state would have to provide for the schooling of nearly a million children, meanwhile facing the church's unabated fury.

The government-proposed school system was frankly anti-Catholic; Azaña, affected by the idealism of the moment, declared that eventually no Spanish child would receive a Catholic education. However, the school-building and teacher-training program hardly got off the ground. Although work was started on fourteen thousand new schools, funds to complete the construction were not forthcoming, and in many areas half-completed buildings were a mute testimony to the Cortes' sluggishness. Furthermore, there was great opposition to the project in some of the heavily Catholic rural municipalities, and there was the ever-present lack of coordination between Madrid and the provinces. The government was frankly hampered by lack of funds, and the teacher-training program was not invigorated.

The church, of course, did not take this challenge passively. It was acutely aware that the constitution called for the termination of teaching by the religious orders; since the church's primary and secondary systems were operated by the orders, the eventual prohibition was to mean a completely new school system for the church as well as the state. The church nurtured a vast educational organization into existence, and lay teachers were recruited for the future replacement of the religious orders. However, it was patently clear that the church would fight the educational laws to the bitter end.

iv

Aside from these religious laws that were not only a burden for the church but for the state as well, for they

12. Ramos-Oliviera, *Politics, Economics and Men,* p. 458.

did not begin to solve the politico-religious problem, the church suffered from a definite national tendency towards anticlericalism. The clergy and practicing Catholics found the fight against anticlericalism a battle that drained their energies because it involved a day-to-day struggle with no assurances of success and no government to appeal to for protection.

This petty anticlericalism served no constructive purpose towards extirpating the church's political influence; indeed, it served to strengthen the church, lending substance to the dictum that religions thrive on persecution. Responsible leaders in the government found it difficult to put an end to this harassment. The municipal governments interpreted the laws as they wished—particularly the urban governments, which were generally in radically anticlerical hands.

For example, the laws secularizing the cemeteries were interpreted in some communities as forbidding religious burials altogether. Religious statues were destroyed with little regard for the wishes of the people; in Bilbao, the anticlerical center of Catholic Vasconia, the *ayuntamiento* decided to tear down a statue of the Sacred Heart in one of the parks. In Seville, two priests were arrested for conducting a funeral procession and charged with violating the law prohibiting public manifestations of religion. One pastor was fined for saying Mass in his church, the roof of which had been destroyed by lightning, as a public display of religion.[13] Priests were fined for allowing "royalistic" music to be played during services and for alluding to the "Kingship of God" in their sermons on the feast of Christ the King. In some towns the tolling of church bells was taxed, in others the wearing of crucifixes as ornamental jewelry was forbidden.[14] The anti-

13. See the discussion on this, *DSCC*, October 31, 1932, p. 9025.
14. Arrarás Iribarren, *Segunda república española*, p, 273.

clericals were having a field day and although the Madrid
government frowned on much of this activity, it took
no active steps to prevent it. All were petty actions, but
they were significant to the Catholics who had voted for
a republic that had promised to respect religion.

More serious was the violence accompanying this anticlericalism. Periodically, on an average of about once a
month, churches were burned or robbed. Often, local
officials made an attempt to guard the churches, but more
often they did not as they never knew when or where
these incidents would occur. No serious attempt was
made to apprehend the incendiaries or robbers; in this, the
government was negligent in view of the strength of its
police forces. Undoubtedly, most of the robberies were
committed by common thieves, and most of the burnings by rabid anticlericals and anarchists, who knew they
could get away with their deeds. Some churches were
completely destroyed and many priceless objects were
burned or stolen.

As a result, the clergy was left with the impression
that it was not healthy to live in a Spain under republican
rule. Catholics reasoned that if the republicans were not
sponsible for the burning and pillaging of their
churches, then they were responsible for having created
a state in which common criminals could commit these
outrages and go unpunished. Many of the clergy's pre-
1931 suspicions were confirmed, and some Catholics began to wonder whether a government that permitted these
abuses could indeed be considered a legally constituted
power.

v

What was the church's reaction to this anticlericalism?
As indicated, there was a widespread feeling of disen-

chantment with the republic by those Catholics who had supported it in 1931. There was also a general movement toward the antirepublican rightist parties and to the quasi-Catholic Acción Nacional. As important in the long run was a spirit of self-criticism that appeared among certain elements within the church. These people began searching for the true root of the religious problem and for the real cause of the church's decline. The weaknesses of the church were discussed openly and solutions were sought. Under the circumstances, this frank self-awareness could only be welcome.

For one thing, the apostasy of the working classes was examined, and numerous studies were published about this phenomenon; the works of Zúñiga and Pieró were indicative of this concern. (See Chapter 5.) Concurrently, attempts were made to place the social problem in its proper perspective, and magazines such as *Cruzada Católica* appeared, devoted to the principles of social justice, appealing to the proletariat and championing their rights, although within the nonviolent limitations of traditional Christian thought.

Catholic political leaders were not silent on this issue. José María Pemán, a monarchist intellectual, admitted that the democratic liberals and socialists had captured the depth of thinking in Spain and that the head and hands of the nation—the intellectuals and the workers—had been alienated from the church.[15] Gil Robles, speaking in Madrid, noted that there were many Catholics who neglected their faith because in the years before the republic they had been lulled into thinking that the official establishment of the church was a substitute for the true practice of religion.[16]

15. *El Siglo Futuro*, January 23, 1933.
16. On June 16, 1932, as quoted in Juan Arrabal, *J. Mª. Gil Robles: Su vida, su actuación, sus ideas* (Madrid, 1933), p. 285.

The Holy See showed a new spirit of conciliation in the appointment of a successor to Cardinal Segura in the See of Toledo. The new primate was Monsignor Isidro Gomá y Tomás, formerly Bishop of Tarrazona. A Catalan, Gomá was a monarchist, but he was also a diplomat. The government was not consulted on his appointment, which came directly from the Vatican.

Gomá was imbued with the new spirit of self-criticism. In a pastoral issued shortly after his installation as Archbishop of Toledo, he acknowledged the church's faults, observing that the great mass of Spaniards lacked deep religious convictions. He deplored the scarcity of both Catholic thought and Christian piety, which feelings, he said, were the result of the laziness and cowardice of many Catholics.[17]

The call for a revival of Catholic intellectualism was met by a group of Catholics who were solidly republican (most supported the republic during the Civil War and were exiled thereafter). These thinkers, led by José Bergamín, Alfredo Mendizábal, and José María Semprún y Gurrea, founded a monthly review, *Cruz y Raya*. The new periodical preached neo-Thomism, and it included articles by such liberal Catholics as Jacques Maritain, Etienne Gilson, and Don Luigi Sturzo.

The new spirit of self-criticism, however, did not mean that Catholics would accept anticlerical legislation; the test was to be met on the floor of the Cortes in the spring of 1933. However, the Spanish church was intellectually more vibrant than it had been ever since the struggles of the nineteenth century began.

vi

During the winter of 1932-33, the floor of the Cortes became the scene of a new and intense struggle between

17. "Horas gravas," in Gomá y Tomás, *Antilaicismo*, I, 237-91.

church and state. The Cortes, after passing a stop-gap agrarian reform law and the Catalan Autonomy Statute, finally turned to the enactment of legislation governing the churches and religious orders in accord with the norms established in the last section of Article 26.

The bill for a Law of Religious Denominations and Congregations, submitted to the Cortes in October of 1932, conformed to Article 26 on most points—registration of the religious orders; prohibition of the orders' educational, industrial, and commercial activities; and regulation of their financial resources—but it added a new feature, although one implicit in other articles of the constitution—the nationalization of church property.

There appear to be a number of reasons why the ministry was particularly anxious to see the law enacted at this time. For one thing, the governing coalition was disintegrating because of the fundamental differences between republicans and Socialists. The ministry wanted the law passed while it still had the power to do so. Furthermore, there is little doubt that the ministry wanted to use the force of anticlericalism to draw the coalition together again; as Gil Robles put it, the bill was "a political stratagem of an unstable government which wanted to give itself an injection of anticlericalism to stay alive."[18] Another reason for the government's haste was that the Cortes had not yet passed the law implementing the Court of Constitutional Guarantees, a safeguard designed to allow an independent tribunal to determine the constitutionality of legislation; the Cortes was determined to legislate against the religious orders before the Catholics could use that recourse.

The Catholic deputies were determined to use every manner of obstructionist tactics to prevent passage of

18. *DSCC*, February 9, 1933, p. 11062.

the bill. They united their forces and planned opposition. The result of this parliamentary conflict was a wearing down of the legislative processes, for although the debates did not begin until February of 1933, they dragged out over a four-month period.

In polemical content, the debates were similar to those which had accompanied every piece of religious legislation. Generally, the Catholic deputies argued that although the bill conformed to Article 26, it was still unjust because Catholics did not consider Article 26 valid; therefore it was useless to appeal to the constitution.

The anticlericals defended the bill using the same arguments they had used before. In the only new argument, Albornoz justified the nationalization of church property by claiming that it had originally belonged to the state, which had leased it to the church. There was, he contended, nothing illegal about the state's reclaiming the land and buildings at this time. Anyway, he argued, nothing would change; the title would pass to the state, but the church would continue to use the land and buildings as before.[19]

The discussion of the law *in toto* ended on March 2, 1933. Then the Cortes went on to discuss and vote separately on each of the thirty-one articles. These debates lasted almost three months; the Catholics used all of their tactics of obstruction. They filibustered on each article to the time limit, called for a quorum vote, and then walked out. They introduced numerous moderating amendments to each article, each requiring a separate vote. For example, when Article 31 (prohibiting the religious orders from teaching) came up for discussion, they offered twenty-eight separate amendments, each exempting one different order from the provisions of the law. Then, when each

19. *DSCC*, March 1, 1933, pp. 11525-34.

of the amendments was discussed, they would eulogize the order to the limit of the time allotted before permitting a vote.[20] The debates proceeded at a snail's pace.

Finally, on May 10, the last article was passed by a vote of 218 to 50, and the Cortes sent the bill to the president for his signature.

The bill was somewhat more extreme than the norms imposed by Article 26.

Articles 1-10 were simply restatements or clarifications of Article 26. Articles 11-19 dealt with church property. All of the property of the church was declared to be the public property of the nation. The church would continue to administer and care for this property, but only the state could dispose of it. The state would decide, in case of conflict, what constituted church property. Religious objects of artistic or historical value could be taken from any church for display in museums. The church would be allowed to acquire private property after the promulgation of the law, but the state could confiscate that property which it did not consider necessary for religious services.

Article 20 recognized the church's right to found and operate seminaries and schools, but the state retained the right to inspect them to guarantee that "within them there will not be taught any doctrine against the security of the Republic."

Article 21 required each religious institution or trust under religious control to submit an annual economic report to the state, which reserved the right of confiscation if it decided these were not pursuing religious aims.

Articles 22-31 dealt with the religious orders. They were required to list with the government all of their *conventos*, the purposes of each, the property owned, and the

20. *DSCC*, May 2, 1933, pp. 12534 ff.

names of all members (two thirds of whom had to be Spanish citizens). They were to submit an annual financial account to the state. They were forbidden to engage in political activity of any type, possess more property than necessary for modest living and personal needs, own rent-producing real estate, or engage in commerce, industry, or agriculture (except to farm enough for their own needs). The state guaranteed its help and protection to any person who wished to leave an order. Finally, the religious orders were forbidden to engage in teaching, either directly or through intermediaries. Orders that violated any of these articles could be dissolved by the Cortes.

At the last moment, the Cortes attached a rider to Article 31. This provision stated that the religious orders were to cease teaching in all secondary schools by October 1, 1933, and in all primary schools by December 31, 1933. As the first of these dates was less than six months away, the Cortes was obviously throwing all caution to the wind, for replacements within this period would be impossible.[21]

Now it was up to the president. With the bill before him, Alcalá Zamora was in a difficult position—the classic position of the Spanish Catholic republican. As president, he had to comply with the Cortes' mandate. As a Catholic he could not violate the church's rights. The only way out of the dilemma would be to veto the bill (which would have freed him from censure by the church), but he knew that the anticlerical bloc in the Cortes had the strength to override his veto, and would certainly do so. Furthermore, the Cortes, in anger, would probably amend the bill

21. The bill is in Soto de Gongoiti, *La iglesia católica y el estado español*, pp. 178-87.

to more radical extremes. The president waited the full twenty days provided by law to think over his decision.

Alcalá Zamora was under great pressure as telegrams, letters, and petitions from Catholics poured into the presidential palace, all urging him to veto the bill. One example was the letter sent in the name of 104 provincial superiors and 4,958 religious communities. These clerics stated that they had always respected the republic in spite of repeated attacks on their persons and property and that they did not demand privileges; they simply asked for justice as Spanish citizens. They reminded the president of his righteous action in resigning over Article 26 in 1931. And, they somberly warned that the regular clergy would suffer martyrdom and bloodshed to continue their work.[22]

What could the president do? If he resigned rather than sign the bill he would withdraw his moderating influence from the government. On the other hand, had his moderating influence ever been effective? The lights burned late in the presidential palace as Alcalá Zamora tried to find his way out of the quandary. But there was no way out, and on June 2 he gave in and signed the bill into law. Protests followed.

The following day, June 3, the Spanish episcopate published a collective declaration. The bishops described the Law of Religious Denominations and Congregations as notoriously unjust and they declared it had no binding power upon Catholics, since the government could not force Catholics to violate the imprescriptable laws of the church. Furthermore, they reminded Catholic parents of their obligation to send their children to Catholic schools, from which duty the faithful could be dispensed only by their bishop. However, the prelates counseled Catholics

22. *A.B.C.*, May 21, 1933.

to work through legal means for the repeal of the law. Finally they cited the articles of canon law pertaining to the excommunication of Catholics who had conscientiously violated Divine Law by legislating against the church.[23]

Did the bishops' citation mean that Alcalá Zamora and the Catholic deputies in the Cortes who had voted for the law were now excommunicates? Catholics were tense and many fully expected an edict, but no formal decree of excommunication was issued.[24] A more important event captured their attention. The following day, for the first time since the republic was proclaimed, Pope Pius XI broke his official silence and issued an encyclical, *Dilectissima nobis,* on the church's condition in Spain.

The Pope discussed the situation in great detail. "With the kindness becoming in a father," he charged that the Law of Religious Denominations and Congregations was an offense against both the church and the civil liberties for which the Spanish government claimed to stand. He noted the church's stand on forms of government: "Let no man suspect, however, that We are in any way influenced by any feeling of aversion towards the new form of government or towards any other innovations of a purely political character, recently introduced in Spain. Everyone knows that the Catholic Church never prefers one form of government over another. All [it] demands is

23. *Ibid.,* June 3, 1933.

24. The president probably did not come under the proscriptions of the cited canon law, for he did not have much choice in the matter and the bishops realized it. And, since no one was named, no one was excommunicated. During the whole period from 1931 to 1936, the church issued only one formal excommunication, that of Canon Luis López Dóriga, dean of the cathedral chapter at Granada, a Cortes deputy who had joined the Radical Socialist party and had refused to oppose any of the religious legislation. He was excommunicated and deprived of his benefice on February 15, 1933, by the Archbishop of Granada. See the *Boletín . . . Sevilla,* April 21, 1933, pp. 99-101.

that, whatever the form of government, the rights of God and of conscience be respected. That done, [it] has no difficulty in getting along with civil institutions, whether they be monarchial, aristocratic, or democratic."

The Pontiff claimed that the government knew that the Spanish episcopate was well disposed toward the constituted authority; thus, he was "amazed" to learn that the church was legislated against under the pretext of the necessity of defending the republic. He could only conclude that the struggle against the church was caused by a "hatred of . . . Christ, nourished by groups subversive to any religious and social order."

Concerning separation of church and state, he remarked that it was an error to assume that it was licit and good in itself and that some nations, having legislated separation, realized their error and either repealed the law or modified their interpretation of it. Civil authority, he stated, suffered from separation; "when the [government] loses the support . . . that sustains it in the conscience of the people, namely the persuasion of its Divine origin, dependence, and sanction, it loses, at the same time its greatest power to obligate."

Pope Pius then charged the government with the following acts of injustice: subjecting the church to the civil power; allowing the "most erroneous opinions" to manifest themselves, while the majority religion was restrained; nationalizing the church's property while forcing it to pay taxes on the same property; ruining the family by the introduction of divorce; depriving the clergy of their salaries, which were a compensation for the *desamortización;* dissolving the Jesuits; and forbidding the religious orders to teach. The legislators, he said, ". . . have defined as extraneous to the Spanish nation the authority of the Vicar of Christ, as if the authority of the Roman

Pontiff . . . could be called extraneous to any part of the world whatsoever; as if the recognition of the Divine Authority of Christ can minimize legitimate human authority; as if the spiritual and supernatural power could be in contrast with that of the State. . . ."

The Pope stated that it was his duty to condemn the law: "We solemnly protest, with all Our strength, against the Law itself, declaring that it cannot be invoked against the inalienable rights of the Church." He called on Spaniards to use all legitimate means, compatible with order and morality, to effect amendment of the law. Finally, the Pontiff called for the faithful to unite: "We again recommend to all Catholic Spain, that laments and recriminations be put aside, and subordinating to the common welfare of Country and Religion every other ideal, all unite . . . to remove the dangers that threaten the civil welfare. . . ."[25]

The government's reaction to these declarations was to begin implementation of the Law of Religious Denominations and Congregations. The Cortes voted an extraordinary education budget of 28,000,000 *pesetas* and the ministry of justice set up machinery to fulfill the Law.[26] Apparently the government was not going to hesitate. Neither did the church, for it immediately began recruiting Catholic certified lay teachers from the state schools for its own system. The deadline for the end of teaching by the religious orders drew closer as the summer came on.

As it turned out, however, there was no need for haste. The Azaña ministry's year-and-a-half struggle to maintain itself in power collapsed in midsummer when the Social-

25. Pius XI, *Dilectissima nobis* (June 3, 1933), published in *Razón y Fe*, 438 (July, 1933), 291-99.
26. *DSCC*, July 26. 1933, p. 14420.

ists withdrew their support. The cause was simply the culmination of grievances between members of the ruling coalition: the republicans felt they had gone far enough, while the Socialists felt they had just started. Makeshift cabinets filled the void for the rest of the summer and early fall until no ministry enjoyed confidence and elections had to be called.

The stage was now set for the swing of the Spanish political pendulum. The struggle with the church had served to alienate the nation's most powerful institution. Many Catholic republicans had deserted the republican parties. The politico-religious conflict had sapped the government's moral strength—a virtue desperately needed by the republicans in their grave struggle with right and left extremists. Finally, the religious strife gave all of the conservative and right-wing groups the one common bond needed to unify them—the defense of Catholicism and of the church's rights.

CHAPTER 11

CEDA AND THE VICTORY
OF THE RIGHT

Manuel Azaña resigned his ministry in September of 1933. The reformer found forces too difficult to deal with. The Socialists had shown their unwillingness to go along with his program, and it became more and more difficult to secure majorities in the Cortes. Of more importance, the president wanted Azaña out of power. Alcalá Zamora had found the affair of the Law of Religious Denominations and Congregations too hot to handle; he did not want to risk the presidential office again. Earlier in the summer, Alcalá Zamora had dismissed Azaña and charged Lerroux with forming a ministry; but Lerroux could not gain the confidence of the Cortes, and Azaña was called back until he resigned in September.

Lerroux again took over while the Cortes was on vacation. When that body reconvened in early October, Lerroux was again refused confidence. The president then offered the premiership to Diego Martínez Barrios, vice chieftain of the Radicals. As the Cortes would not vote confidence in Martínez Barrios either, Alcalá Zamora dissolved the Cortes and called elections for November 19, 1933. In the interim Martínez Barrios ruled.

With the Radicals in control of the ministry, no definite program of action could be effected. Everyone awaited the electoral mandate, and only half-hearted attempts were made to enforce the Republican-Socialist reform legislation. The Law of Religious Denominations and Congregations was not enforced. As the October deadline for the cessation of teaching by the religious orders approached, the state had only 77 new schools to replace the 300 *colegios* it planned to close, and only 611 new teachers to replace the 2,050 clerical instructors.[1] Many of the religious schools began closing their doors, but October 1 came and went without an official closing order. On borrowed time, the regular clergy went back to their teaching duties.

By mid-October the electoral campaign occupied the nation's attention. The parties of the right had been preparing for this day for two years. While the republicans and Socialists had been busy legislating and struggling with each other, the rightists had had ample time to unify their forces and to begin their appeals to the Spanish electorate. As its unifying theme the right seized upon the religious issue and it raised its banner in the defense of the church. With this bond, the right became a formidable political power.

i

The single most important rightist party was the moderate Catholic organization, Acción Nacional. Ever since the passage of the constitution it had been developing its

1. *El Debate*, September 23, 1933.

resources. It still claimed to be an organization—not a party—composed of Catholics whose aim was to defend the church and for whom the question of form of government was secondary. Despite these claims Acción Nacional had developed into a highly organized political party. Its name had been changed to Acción Popular (when the government forbade the use of the word *nacional* for political parties), and it was now the parent of a number of other organizations designed to appeal to special groups within the moderate Catholic ranks—such as Acción Femenina, Acción Obrerista, and the youth organization, Juventudes de Acción Popular. The primary aim of all these groups was the same as that of the parent —"defense of the social order and the rights of religion."

Gil Robles, president of Acción Popular, had not changed his views on the politico-religious question; he clarified them in a speech of June 16, 1932.[2] He stated that while in pure theory the church and the state are perfect societies and the church is superior because of the higher nature of its end (and thus the state should be subordinated to the church), the practical state of affairs was quite different. Under the present circumstances, he contended, all that Catholics asked for were liberty and the recognition of the independence and juridic personality of the church.

How did he intend to bring this about? Through political action. His organization, he said, would take three steps to secure the church's rights. First, Catholics were to ignore the question of form of government, for this was a "secondary question when the social order . . . is threatened." Second, Catholics were to submit to the constituted power, while at the same time making the distinction between form of government (the republic)

2. In Arrabal, *Gil Robles*, pp. 285-92.

and unjust legislation (the religious laws). Finally, the fight against the religious laws was to be within the framework of legality: "I am totally opposed to a military conspiracy to overthrow the State," he declared. The legal fight, he claimed, would help Spaniards adjust to the life of democratic citizens.

Gil Robles' position was, of course, dictated by circumstances. He could make no declaration concerning the form of government because most of his followers had a marked preference for a monarchy, and they would have deserted him had he declared for the republic. On the other hand, he could not publicly declare in favor of a monarchy and expect to appeal to the electorate. It required the consummate skill of a master politician to walk this tightrope. How well he succeeded can be seen by the rise and fall of his political star in the following years.

On October 22, 1932, representatives of Acción Popular and its affiliates met to form a new political organization, the Confederación Española de Derechas Autónomas, or the CEDA. In effect, the CEDA was simply Acción Popular with a broader base; its leaders and organizational structure were the same.

The CEDA's platform was centered on the "restoration of religious rights." In this regard, it called for a repeal of the civil marriage and divorce laws, complete freedom of education, including the right of the religious orders to teach, and negotiations for a concordat with the Holy See.

The CEDA's social program was based on papal social teaching, particularly Leo XIII's *Rerum novarum* and Pius XI's *Quadragesimo anno*. Thus, it called for a more equitable distribution of wealth and the intervention of the state in economic-social matters, although it rejected the Marxist principle of class warfare. The *cedistas* wanted absolute freedom of labor, just wages, profit sharing, and government-directed bargaining boards. In agrarian matters, their platform called for the creation of a small landowner class, through the cession of state and municipally owned lands, and from lands expropriated from the large landowners, with just compensation.[3]

How much of its economic and social program did the CEDA intend to effect? Although there were many sincere social reformers in its ranks, and although Gil Robles had stated that "we cannot talk to the landowners of their rights but rather of their obligations,"[4] the cold fact was that the *cedistas* were dependent on the landowners. The grain-producing oligarchy of the central tableland, opportunistic, with no particular political program save one committed to saving their own wealth, was one of CEDA's strongest supports. The CEDA needed money to win the election, for it was planning a high-pressure campaign;[5] the oligarchy was willing to donate, as long as it was assured that the expropriation of their lands would remain a dead letter.

From the beginning, the CEDA's idealistic program was burdened with the oligarchy's dead weight. It remained so for the rest of its existence. Everyone knew about the CEDA-oligarchic alliance, but the *cedistas* continued to talk of agrarian reform as if they had made no political concessions or commitments. It was sheer hypocrisy, but for Gil Robles there was no choice; victory would come only with the political support of the pro-

3. For the CEDA's entire program, see José Monge y Bernal, *Acción popular: Estudio de biología política* (Madrid, 1936), pp. 478, 486-87, 670-801.

4. *Cruzada Católica,* November, 1932, p. 5.

5. Brenan, *Spanish Labyrinth,* p. 268, notes that before 1931 the spoils system had provided the necessary incentive for political campaigns.

letariat and the economic support of the oligarchy. A deformity was born within the body politic.

ii

The other rightist groups, aside from the government parties—Maura's Republican Right and the Radicals—were concentrated into four parties.

The Agrarian party was the one most closely allied with the CEDA. Indeed, Gil Robles had been elected to the Cortes in 1931 as an Agrarian. It was the party of the landed oligarchs of north-central Spain. Its leaders were willing to side with any group that would return Spain to the socio-economic *status quo* of 1930. Its religious program called for "the restoration of the Church's rights" but mentioned no specific points.

The Basque Nationalists were another rightist party. Their peculiar political development centered completely on demands for regional autonomy. They were violently opposed to the religious legislation, but they supported the republic otherwise, for the republic provided the means for autonomy. The Republican-Socialists had not been so quick to act upon the Basque's demands as they had for the Catalans. According to the constitution, autonomy had to undergo the test of a regional plebiscite. In fact, during these same months—the fall of 1933—the Basques were campaigning in their own provinces; the Autonomy Statute won overwhelming approval in the three provinces of Álava, Viscaya, and Guipúzcoa on November 5, 1933.[6] The Cortes, however, was not in session, pending the election, so no action had yet been taken. The Basque Nationalists then, although proclerical on the religious question, were far to the left in their separatist demands. On

6. Bishop Múgica had been allowed to return to Spain in 1933, and he warmly supported the Autonomy Statute—much to the dismay of the rest of the episcopate.

economic and social matters they took no stand, for the social problem in Vasconia was not extreme.

The two other rightist groups—the Alfonsists and the Traditionalists—were both monarchist. The Traditionalists had been planning to overthrow the republic by force ever since 1931, but in 1932 they had formed a political party, the Communión Tradicionalista Carlista. Their political and religious programs were identical: they wanted the Carlist pretender to rule as king with the support of the clergy—not far from a pure theocracy. The Traditionalists were, of course, completely opposed to the religious laws and to the republic as well. In the mountain strongholds of Navarre, one did not have to go far to find the *requetés* drilling; their leaders were in constant communication with the disgruntled army officers who were also planning armed insurrection.

The other monarchist group, the Alfonsists, were also in communication with the Traditionalists, to the extent that dynastic differences were set aside for the time being in favor of an all-out assault on the republic. The Alfonsists had organized as a party, Renovación Española, mainly through the efforts of Antonio Goicoechea, a former *cedista*. Its main source of strength was the army and the aristocracy. Its most important leaders were Ramiro de Maeztu, Eugenio Vegas Latapié, and José Calvo Sotelo. The latter was their outstanding politician; he had been minister of finance under Primo de Rivera and was now living in Paris as an exile.

Renovación Española's religious program was an integral part of its political platform, for it felt that Spain could survive only under the monarchy, in union with the church as it had before 1931. The royalists, along with the Traditionalists, disliked the CEDA intensely and accused the moderate Catholics of warping papal doctrine to suit their own needs. Vegas Latapié, for example, argued that the papal approach to church-state problems as formulated by Leo XIII in the French struggles of the 1880's could not be applied to Spain (as the *cedistas* were doing) because Spain had deeper monarchial roots than the French had had.[7]

Renovación Española would use any means to achieve a restoration, but its leaders hoped to do so legally, by winning a majority in the Cortes. However, others within its ranks were not so sanguine, and they lent their support to a military insurrection in Seville in August, 1932, led by General José Sanjurjo (not a monarchist). The uprising was put down and many of the royalists were arrested and sent to a penal colony in Africa. Those who escaped the arrests fled to France where they came into contact with their French counterparts, Charles Maurras and Léon Daudet, leaders of the papal-banned *Action Française*. There occurred a fruitful exchange of ideas.

Not a major rightist party at this time, but none the less important, was the Fascist party, the Falange Española. Its founder and organizer was José Antonio Primo de Rivera, son of the dictator. In 1933, it was a small party, whose main support came from university students.

The Falange's religious program was tied up with its intense nationalism. It called for the defense of Catholicism, not for any spiritual reason, but because it viewed the church as an integral element of national unity; a Spain without Catholicism was unthinkable. Church leaders however, were skeptical of the new party's chances for success and refused to lend it support. They were counting on the CEDA to lead Spain out of the politico-religious problem. Thus, the Falange and the CEDA became bitter enemies.

7. *Catolicismo y república* (Madrid, 1932).

This was the political spectrum of the right. They all had one element in common: despite the wide range of the parties, from the quasi-republicanism of the CEDA to the theocracy of the Traditionalists, all incorporated the defense of the church into their platforms.

iii

Rightist political strength had been evident long before the elections of November, 1933. Indeed, some of the Cortes deputies felt that Azaña should have resigned in April, 1933, when municipal elections were held in those towns that had returned monarchist councilors in the elections of April, 1931. Although these municipalities were, in Azaña's terms, *burgos podridos* and had well-known conservative leanings, the results of the elections surprised the ministry. The Agrarians outpolled all other parties, with the Radicals and Socialists running second and third.

In September of 1933, the rightists showed their strength again when they won over the Republican-Socialists by three to one in the elections for the newly established Court of Constitutional Guarantees. Although these elections were neither popular nor direct—the *ayuntamientos,* the faculties of the law, and the college of lawyers chose the court—they clearly indicated a trend.

Therefore, when the electoral campaign for the new Cortes began in earnest in October, the right felt confident, for the left was disunited. More perceptive members of the left warned of the consequences of disunion, especially in view of the electoral law that they themselves had legislated, but to no avail. Three different lists of candidates appeared as the remains of what had once been the Republican-Socialist coalition.

The right, on the other hand, had learned from experience. They had suffered from disunion in the 1931 elections; they now put aside differences to present a unified slate. On October 15, the CEDA, the Agrarians, Renovación Española, and the Communión Tradiciona- lista published a manifesto announcing the formation of a common front. They called for repeal of the "laic and socialist laws, defense of agrarian rights and the pardon of all political prisoners."[8] This was a specious program and left much unsaid; as a matter of fact, little could be said. The form of government was not mentioned, for this was a touchy point. However, the monarchists were certainly planning for the restoration of the monarchy should the right coalition win, and they felt certain that the CEDA would support them in this regard.

The CEDA made no commitments, but a speech Gil Robles had made the previous November in Valencia was significant. At that time, the CEDA leader had stated that the CEDA would work within the legal framework of the republic should it come to power.[9] However, much had transpired since 1932, particularly the Law of Reli- gious Denominations and Congregations. Certainly, the monarchists felt, Gil Robles had changed his mind; but the CEDA leader was noncommittal at the beginning of the campaign.

If the right coalition could not agree on the question of form of government, they did agree on the importance of the religious problem; indeed, it was their common bond. Gil Robles frankly admitted this when he stated that "if the religious issue should disappear, each of us would go his own way."[10]

The right had some difficulty at first in achieving har- mony, so tenuous were the bonds that united the different

8. *A.B.C.*, October 15, 1933.
9. *El Debate*, November 30, 1932.
10. *A.B.C.*, October 20, 1933.

parties. In the urban centers of the northern provinces, where the Agrarians ruled the countryside, the right was joined by the Radicals, despite the latter's traditional anticlericalism. The monarchists opposed them, almost to the point of breaking the coalition, but the *cedistas* successfully defended them as running mates.

In Madrid, the Falange made a bid to join the coalition, but was asked to withdraw; Gil Robles had no use for this small Fascist party that could give only trouble. Primo de Rivera ran independently.

Why had the *cedistas* made a pact with the monarchists? Simply because they could not afford to risk losing the election. They needed money to run the campaign and the monarchists had money. For the first time in a Spanish election the radio was used extensively and airplanes were hired to drop electoral propaganda all over Spain. The CEDA could not afford this type of campaign, so it had to ally with the monarchists and the oligarchy, especially since it could not offer the electorate a solid promise of reform.

One thing offered hope to the right; the electorate had been doubled through the granting of the franchise to women. Generally, the female vote was considered to be more conservative, since they were usually more active church-goers than men. But this was only conjecture and not yet substance.

Officially, the clergy remained fairly silent during the campaign. Cardinal Ilundáin ordered prayers, "in consideration of the situation the Church is in . . . with elections approaching,"[11] but no pastoral was written by any of the bishops. Either they were certain that the right would be victorious or else they wanted to give no cause for offense at this crucial time. The only reported inci-

11. *Boletín* . . . *Sevilla,* November 7, 1933, p. 273.

dent occurred in Valencia, where the civil government protested to the archbishop that some of the clergy were preaching politics and asked that they be reprimanded. The archbishop replied that perhaps some people were reading too much into the sermons and that all of his priests were loyal to the regime.[12] The only official statement from Acción Católica (now under the presidency of Herrera Oria, who had resigned his position on the staff of *El Debate*) was a reminder that "Catholics are obliged to vote against the implementation of the antireligious laws."[13]

As the campaign warmed, Gil Robles' star rose. He averaged three major speeches a week during the monthlong campaign, more than any other person, left or right. In his enthusiasm he compromised himself with statements that he was to spend the rest of his political life attempting to live down. He declared in unequivocal terms that the right was going to create a new state, regardless of the sacrifice: "We want integral power. . . . Until we get it we will not collaborate with anyone. To realize this idea, we are not going to be deterred by archaic forms. For us, democracy is a means, not an end. . . . When the time arrives, [the Cortes] will submit to us or we will do away with it."[14]

This theme was repeated in other speeches. He warned the left that if they acted against the popular mandate in the event of a right victory, he also would move out of the democratic framework to effect his program. He stated that he wanted a strong, powerful government that would "follow traditional Spanish thought, but which would preserve personal liberties." On the eve of the election he declared that the CEDA did not want

12. *A.B.C.*, October 19, 1933.
13. *Ibid.*, November 12, 1933.
14. *El Debate*, October 17, 1933.

the violence of either the masses or the tyrant: "We wish to be between the democracy that separates and the dictatorship that menaces."[15]

Was it any wonder then, that the leftists feared the end of the republic if the CEDA took over? The left cried, "Fascism!" and Gil Robles was lampooned in their press, adorned with a Hitlerian moustache and a blackshirt. Later events proved that Gil Robles was carried away by enthusiasm, but the monarchists heartily approved his speeches.

The Republican-Socialists condemned Gil Robles and concentrated on the theme that the right was going to do away with the republic. They defended their reforms and the religious laws. For example, Marcelino Domingo noted that the republic had been quiet and orderly until "Segura declared war on us. . . . [His] pastoral turned the course of the Republic." De los Ríos said that Spanish Catholics had never been Christians and never could be, for Spanish Catholicism was incompatible with true Christianity. Felipe Sánchez Román, a conservative republican, contended that there had been no religious persecution and that such events as the expulsion of the Jesuits had been of only "momentary consequence."[16]

These statements were not designed to win Catholic support, but the left was not concerned with the Catholics; they hoped to rally the anticlericals to their side. Lerroux, however, struck a discordant note. The Radical leader who had led the attacks on the churches in the *semana trágica*, the man who in all of his life had been loyal to only one ideal—anticlericalism—declared that the

15. *El Debate*, November 3, 1933; *A.B.C.*, November 14 and November 19, 1933.

16. Domingo's speech is in *El Liberal*, October 24, 1933; De los Ríos' is in *El Socialista*, October 24, 1933; Sánchez Román's is in *El Debate*, November 12, 1933.

government's religious policy had been a mistake: "Laicism should not consist of torturing the religious conscience of the country; laicism should leave no one discontented."[17] Spaniards shook their heads in wonderment; the republic had produced more than bargained for!

As the tempo of the campaign was stepped up, the right's propaganda became so intense that the ministry grounded all leaflet-dropping planes, and early on election eve it decreed a halt to political broadcasting. By then it had become apparent that the disunited left had little chance of winning. Furthermore, the anarcho-syndicalists had been ordered by their leaders to stay away from the polls; they would have no more of moderate reforms; they wanted a revolution. This meant that the left would lose the support of a large group that had voted for them in 1931.

On Sunday, November 19, the people of Spain elected a new Cortes. Although in terms of the popular vote, the right (not including the center) outpolled the left by only a few thousand votes, the law of proportional representation gave the right a great victory. The right coalition won 192 seats, with the 25 seats won by independent rightists; its bloc numbered 217 deputies. Of these the CEDA had 115, the Agrarians 36, and the monarchist groups 45 among them. The center won 163 seats, with the Radicals holding 102 of these. The left's total was 93; of these the Socialists had 60, and Azaña's Left Republicans returned only 5 deputies.

Why had the left lost? A number of factors must be taken into consideration. The most obvious reason was the disunion between republicans and Socialists. The abstention of the anarcho-syndicalists meant the loss of nearly half a million votes. The female vote, normally

17. *El Debate*, November 10, 1933.

conservative, added to the right's total. Furthermore, a large conservative republican sector of opinion felt that the Constituent Cortes had illegally stayed in session after formulating the constitution, and they registered their protest by voting against the left.

Another important factor was the Radicals' desertion of the democratic liberal cause; this meant more than appeared on the surface, for the Radicals controlled the ministry. Martínez Barrios and Lerroux made certain that men who could deliver the vote to the center and the right were appointed as governors of the various provinces; in this revival of *caciqueismo* they had the collusion of the president.

However, the strength of the right should not be underestimated. The CEDA's superb organization and Gil Robles' unifying ability—Machiavellian that it was— proved to be a major factor in its victory. Because the bond of unity of the right had been the defense of the church, the Republican-Socialist religious policy had carried within itself the seeds of political defeat.

CHAPTER 12

THE CHURCH AND THE BIENIO NEGRO

The two years from December, 1933, to December, 1935, have come to be known in Spanish history as the *bienio negro* (black biennium). This sobriquet, bestowed by right and left alike, is descriptive of the paralysis of official action and the repeal or nonenactment of much of the Republican-Socialist reform legislation. The basic cause of this paralysis was an imbalance of government, resulting in ministerial instability, which, in turn, resulted from two factors: the disunion of the right and the left's distrust of the CEDA. The root of the problem in both cases was the question of form of government. The right was divided because the monarchists wanted a restoration, while the CEDA wanted to maintain the republic. The left distrusted the CEDA because it feared that the oligarchy's control of the CEDA would spell the death of the spirit of republican reform, if not of the republic itself.

The politico-religious problem was the root of the question of form of government. Gil Robles attempted to force his solution upon the government; the religious laws were not implemented. These actions brought about accusations of antirepublicanism from the left, for the reformers saw their constitution violated. Once having accomplished their religious aims, the *cedistas* had no further plan, for their commitments to the oligarchy nullified any social and agrarian reform. Because of the CEDA's actions and the division over form of government, there was a deep distrust of each party for every other. The result was a standstill in the government.

i

The right coalition's immediate reaction to the results of the elections was joyful, for allied with the center, it commanded a clear majority in the Cortes and could presumably effect its political program. But, what was its program? The right's election manifesto was ambiguous, and there had been a misunderstanding of party aims long before November. This confusion centered on the CEDA and ultimately prevented a parliamentary union.

The monarchists (both Renovación Española and the Communión Tradicionalista) wanted the CEDA to declare itself antirepublican. Gil Robles had certainly compromised himself enough in his campaign speeches, so that he could have done so without difficulty. With the CEDA firmly among the antirepublicans, the monarchists felt that a united right could then refuse collaboration to any ministry, which would force new elections. Another election, they felt, could win them a majority antirepublican Cortes, which body would then declare a restoration and return Alfonso XIII to power.

This scheme was probably palatable to most of the

cedistas, but whether or not it was feasible or could be effected without bloodshed was another question. The monarchists had high hopes and Calvo Sotelo, returned from exile, publicly advocated this plan. In an obvious reference to the CEDA, he commented that any right party that did not declare itself antirepublican would be defrauding the will of the electorate.[1]

Gil Robles, however, saw the fallacies of the monarchists' project. An attempt to restore the king would result in civil war and proletarian revolution. Already, anarchists in some of the small Catalan villages were burning churches and proclaiming *communismo libertario* simply because of the election results. Gil Robles could not effect his plans without domestic peace; violence was not conducive to a settlement of the religious problem. Therefore, he began to lead the CEDA to complete acceptance of the republic.

He gave indications of this drift in early December, before the new Cortes met. In an interview with a French reporter, he stated that the CEDA accepted the constituted power according to the church's teachings, and he hoped the royalists would not endanger a peaceful solution to the problem.[2] A few days later he announced that he was withdrawing the CEDA from the right coalition for it was not yet time for the right to govern.[3]

Gil Robles' immediate problem was the makeup of the new Cortes. Although the CEDA was the largest party, it had less than half of a total majority; if it declared itself republican, the monarchists would not join it in a coalition. Thus, there was no possibility of a right majority coalition. On the other hand, the disunited left

1. Galindo Herrero, *Los partidos monárquicos,* p. 103.
2. *A.B.C.,* December 1, 1933.
3. *El Sol,* December 7, 1933.

could not govern, for it commanded scarcely one-fourth of the deputies. It appeared that only the Radicals, the strongest party of the center, could form a ministry, relying on either the left or right for support. A Radical-left coalition was out of the question, for not only were the two opposed (the left had principles, if not political acumen), but the CEDA threatened to ally with the monarchists to prevent such a ministry. Therefore, the Radicals had to ally with the right, specifically the CEDA. Would the CEDA support them?

Gil Robles was prepared to offer support, for if he did not the only alternative would be elections, unpredictable at best. On the other hand, there was the possibility that he could, in time, control the Radicals; Lerroux had been bought before. If this was corruption, Gil Robles had compromised with corruption before; now, he felt, it offered the only real hope for a peaceful solution to the politico-religious problem.

Therefore, on December 15, after a week of presidential consultations to form a ministry, *El Debate* announced that the moderate Catholics would not support any movement, legal or illegal, to overthrow the republic. Noting that the church could live under any form of government, the CEDA's organ stated that the republican form was not responsible for the religious laws and that it was possible to be both a good republican and a good Catholic.[4]

The monarchists were livid with rage. They had not joined in the right coalition to see the republic preserved. The leaders of Renovación Española declared that they were willing to go along with the republic until things got settled, but only to smooth the path for a restoration; the CEDA's acceptance of the republican form was incom-

4. Editorial of December 15, 1933.

prehensible; a republic never had advantages over a monarchy, especially the Spanish monarchy. The Traditionalists were even more disturbed, particularly by *El Debate*'s near-pontifical tone of authority. "By what perversion of papal thought," they asked, "are Catholics supposed to prefer a republic to the monarchy?" Especially, the Second Republic. "How can one convince a partisan of the glorious Spanish Monarchy that the [Second] Republic will last when the First Republic disappeared like snow in the sun?"[5]

On the other hand, most leftists dismissed *El Debate*'s statement as political maneuvering because they felt that under the CEDA only the name of the republic would last; what it had stood for would not. The Socialist press dryly noted that it was about time Rome recognized the permanence of the republic, "after its dealings with the bloody regimes in Italy and Germany."[6]

Gil Robles agreed to support a Radical ministry, and Lerroux became premier again. He made it clear that he was not going to collaborate formally with the Radicals nor accept a ministerial position but simply that the CEDA would give Lerroux's ministry a vote of confidence. Defending his position in the opening session of the new Cortes, he said that the CEDA did not want to govern because "the wounds we have received are too recent, and we cannot answer that a spirit of vengeance would not carry us away." Following this ominous statement, he confessed that he had sorrowfully seen the republic come in, but he had learned to live with it, and his position now was one of loyal adherence to the republic. His main task, he said, would be to work for constitutional revision,

5. *El Siglo Futuro*, December 16 and 25, 1933.
6. *El Socialista*, December 16, 1933.

but before anything else, he wanted a legislative program "to restore the Church's rights."[7]

Gil Robles amplified his views to the press later in the day. He warned that the CEDA would vote no credits for the educational budget until the law forbidding teaching by the religious orders was repealed. His support of the republic, he said, was not a question of regime but of religion. He would facilitate a center government now, but when the time was propitious, the CEDA would claim full power: "To those who say I have been insincere, I answer that everything I am doing is to save the Church."[8]

His plan was apparent. He would keep the Radical ministry in power by supporting it on most issues; in return, he would demand that the Radicals support his religious legislation. In time, when he felt that the left would accept his entry into the ministry, he would demand the premiership. From that position, he would spearhead the plan for constitutional revision. If he were refused this post, he would prevent the formation of any ministry and force elections. He probably could have realized these aims had it not been for one important factor—the undying hostility of the president. Alcalá Zamora was determined never to admit the young Catholic leader to power.

Lerroux was, of course, glad to have the support of the CEDA. His previous sojourn as premier had given him the taste of power; furthermore from this position he could reward with political patronage the many *compadres* who had supported him through the years. That

7. *Diario de las sessiones de las cortes: Congreso de los diputados;* December 19, 1933, pp. 74-79. Hereafter cited as *DSC*. The Agrarian leader, José Martínez de Velasco, joined the CEDA in supporting Lerroux. Except for social legislation, the Agrarians supported CEDA policy for the following two years.

8. *La Gaceta Regional* (Salamanca), December 20, 1933.

his militant anticlericalism had to give way bothered him not in the least. His speech of acceptance in the Cortes was pure doubletalk. He announced that he would respect the legislative work of the Constituent Cortes "from the laic laws to the regional statutes;" however, he would support the nation's wishes in regard to the religious laws. Only Lerroux could do both! The following day he said that the termination of teaching by the religious orders could not be implemented within the time limit of December 31.[9]

It is easy to condemn Lerroux; his demagoguery, corruption, and opportunism were approached by no Spaniard; they have been approached by few politicians in any country in the course of history. No honest historian can defend him in this regard. Yet, Lerroux was possessed of political acumen, and he saw what the democratic liberals did not—that the republic could be firmly consolidated only by a moderate center government that could absorb the Catholics.[10] It was Lerroux's personal tragedy—and he was a tragic person for he had the seeds of political greatness within him—that his Radical party lacked the moral strength to offer both moderation and reform. A true center party could have offered stability, but Lerroux's could not, for his political fortunes were built upon the quicksands of corruption.

In any event, his ministry was in an extremely precarious position; the Radicals ruled for the next two years only because Alcalá Zamora supported them. There were constant attacks from left and right extremists, alike in their justifiable hatred of the center. Furthermore the CEDA was a thorn in Lerroux's flesh, for it enjoyed greater power out of the ministry than it would have had had it

9. *DSC*, December 19, 1933, p. 74; December 20, 1933, pp. 116-22.
10. Lerroux, *La pequeña historia*, p. 393.

controlled the government (where it would have been forced to please every party, instead of making the ministry please it). Given these conditions, it is indeed a wonder that the nation survived the *bienio negro*.

ii

The CEDA's prime interest was religious legislation. With a fairly free hand given by the Radicals in return for support, they turned their attention to three problems that they felt demanded immediate consideration: clerical salaries, religious education, and the status of the religious orders.

State-paid clerical salaries had terminated in 1933 in accordance with Article 26. The law was absolutely clear on this point; the state was to make no more payments to the clergy. The CEDA sought for a way to extend the payments without having to face a constitutional test. Gil Robles' solution was simple: the clergy had been employees of the state before 1931; therefore, as retired civil servants they were entitled to pensions.

When he introduced a bill to this effect, providing for pensions to all clergy over forty years of age, equal to two-thirds of their 1931 salaries, there occurred a curious reversal of positions. The anticlericals, who in 1931 had argued that the clergy were state employees (and thus separation meant the termination of salaries), now argued otherwise. The rightists, who in 1931 had contended that salaries were a compensation for the *desamortización*, now claimed that the clergy had indeed been civil servants.

The debates on the bill were characterized by the same polemical oratory that had accompanied all previous religious legislation. The leftists tried to delay passage by using many of the same tactics the right had used the year before, but they were unable to hold out for long. At the final vote they walked out. The tally was 271 to 6.[11] This law awarded those clergy who had been in legal possession of their parishes on December 11, 1931, an annuity equal to two-thirds of their 1931 salary, except that those who had received more than 7,000 *pesetas* in 1931 were to receive no benefits. For 1934 and 1935, 16,500,000 *pesetas* were voted into the budget each year for this purpose. According to the ministry of justice, in 1935 there were 23,083 clergy receiving aid, each averaging about 2,000 *pesetas* ($300) annually. As the stipends were given only to these specific priests, it was planned that as they gradually died, the clerical budget would become smaller, and it would be extinguished completely at the end of one generation.

In justice, what can be said? On the one hand, this law appeared to be a clear violation of the spirit of the constitution. On the other, the constitution had been unnecessarily harsh on those clergy who had no other source of income. The law provided a moderate solution to the problem of clerical salaries, and at the same time was designed to end the problem altogether within a generation.

The next immediate religious problem was the teaching status of the religious orders. A decree of December 30, 1933, suspended the enactment of the Law of Religious Denominations and Congregations in this regard. This appeared to be all that the CEDA could do. When the educational budget for 1934 was discussed in June of that year the religious orders were still teaching, and the CEDA felt that it could vote the credits. However, it refused the minister of public instruction the funds for a study of the replacement of the regular clergy. Even with this restriction, the budget for public instruction

11. See the debates, *DSC*, March 17, 1934, through April 4, 1934.

in 1934 was 311,000,000 *pesetas* (as compared with 296,000,000 in 1933, and 255,000,000 in 1932). In 1935, 345,000,000 *pesetas* was voted, with the same restrictions regarding the substitution of the religious orders.[12]

The only part of the Law of Religious Denominations and Congregations which was strictly enforced was that requiring the religious orders to register with the ministry of justice. Most of the other articles were not implemented; as early as December 7, 1933, the prohibition against the sale of property by the orders was suspended. Furthermore, with a strong spokesman in the Cortes, the episcopate made it officially clear that there were some sections of the law by which it would not abide. Cardinal Ilundáin sent a note to the regular clergy in his diocese reminding them that no one was to be allowed into their cloisters without the express permission of the archbishop or the provincial superior.[13]

The Jesuit expropriation commission, which had been nationalizing Jesuit property ever since the spring of 1932, found its activities limited; a decree of September 27, 1934, confined its investigations only to that property actually registered in the name of the Society of Jesus. The commission had little to do after this decree.

The left's demise did not mean that official anticlericalism was dead. Many of the towns still remained under the control of anticlerical *ayuntamientos.* The state schools still taught a rigid laicism. In Catalonia especially, where the anticlerical Esquerra remained in control, there was no abatement of anticlericalism. However, in all of Spain, the civil guard took on the active protection of churches from acts of violence. Churches were still burned—in

12. See the debates in *Congreso de los diputados: Extracto oficial,* June 26, 1934, through June 29, 1934. Hereafter cited as *CDE.* For 1935, see *CDE,* June 27, 1935, ff.

13. *Boletín . . . Sevilla,* December 12, 1933, p. 296.

December, 1933, in Zaragoza and Granada; during the October revolution of 1934; and during Holy Week, 1935, in Zaragoza—but these were the only acts of anticlerical vandalism during the *bienio negro*. Furthermore, many of the religious laws were relaxed. Civil authorities granted permission for the annual Corpus Christi and Holy Week processions to be held publicly throughout Spain in 1934 and 1935. The minister of public instruction re-established many of the church holy days as school holidays.

The episcopate and the Holy See breathed easier; it appeared that Gil Robles had justified their support of him. But many wiser persons were disturbed, for there was appearing among the left a profound feeling of vengeance. As the prisons filled with anarcho-syndicalists, jailed for acts of industrial violence, bitterness between right and left was exacerbated. There would be no quarter given if the left ever returned to full power.

iii

The CEDA intended to fulfill one important electoral promise—negotiations for a concordat with the Holy See. The Radicals did not look askance at this move, for they knew that nothing would come of the negotiations. The Cortes would have to approve of any accord, and the Radicals could have blocked ratification if necessary; meanwhile, by agreeing to the negotiations, they would continue to enjoy the CEDA's support. In reality, church-state relations were so unstable that a concordat was an impossibility.

The Holy See would not agree to an accord without ample assurance that the religious laws would be repealed or made permanently noneffective. The CEDA could not give this assurance because it was not inherently strong; its power was derived from its parliamentary position of

the moment. The Spanish political situation was too un-
settled and another election, at any time, could return the
left to power. If this happened, a concordat would simply
be another provocation to anticlericalism. Furthermore,
by 1934 papal concordatory policy had received setbacks
in Germany and Italy, and the Pope was not willing to
take risks again. Even in a socially and politically stable
nation a concordat is difficult to effect; in Spain it would
have been impossible. However, the Holy See entered
into negotiations in order to specify the conditions for an
accord should the time be propitious in the future.
Furthermore, negotiations would help to bolster Gil
Robles' position with Spanish Catholics and also give
substance to the thesis that it was possible to be both a
good Catholic and a good republican.

The situation called for a good Catholic, a good republican, and an able diplomat to go to Rome, for the
negotiations would also provide a source of information.
A young Galician independent, Leandro Pita Romero, the
foreign minister in the Lerroux ministry and a personal
friend of Alcalá Zamora, was named ambassador to the
Holy See. That Pita Romero retained his post as foreign
minister made his mission seem more important than it
actually was.

The Holy See did not immediately approve Pita
Romero's nomination. This delay gave the foreign minister an opportunity to display both his impatience and
republicanism. In February, 1934, after the nuncio had
delivered a sermon in the Madrid Cathedral on the occasion of the Pope's birthday, pointing to the "sad situation
in which Spain the unfortunate first child of the papacy
. . . has tried to put up a bold front of glory under a laic
republic," Pita Romero delivered a protest to the Holy See
denouncing Tedeschini's use of state buildings to attack

the government.[14] Apparently, Pita Romero used the incident to display his anticlerical republicanism, to convince the left that, whatever course the negotiations took,
he would remain loyal to the republic.

The affair was smoothed over, and by the end of the
month Pita Romero received his *placet*. However, not
until June did he arrive in Rome. Perhaps he himself
wondered what the point of his journey was.[15] During the
summer, various reports and rumors indicated some of the
issues at stake: the re-establishment of the Tribunal de la
Rota (the church's court of annulment proceedings), in-
demnity claims for the 1931 church burnings, and the government's wish to be consulted in the naming of the higher
clergy.

His mission was further complicated by visits of the
Basque and Catalan Catholics to Rome, both trying to
arrange separate concordats. The Holy See was in no
position to honor their requests; had it done so, it would
have tacitly been recognizing Catalan and Basque autonomy.

In January, 1935, the Pope named six new Spanish
bishops, with the exception of the primate the first to be
appointed since 1930. Officially, the government had no
say on the appointments, but unofficially Pita Romero was
certainly consulted. This was one mark of concord between the two powers, but throughout 1935, the negotiations became less frequent and less meaningful.

On November 21, 1935, Pope Pius announced that

14. For the nuncio's sermon, see Tedeschini, *Discursos y cartas,*
pp. 124-30, and *A.B.C.,* February 18 and 20, 1934.

15. See *El Socialista,* June 1, 1934, for the rumor that the nuncio
telephoned the Holy See and told them to stall Pita Romero until the
political situation changed. The incident is unlikely because the nuncio
did not have to tell the Vatican what it already knew; if he had, he
certainly would not have been indiscreet enough to telephone. On the
other hand, none of the rightist papers denied the incident.

Tedeschini and Gomá were to be elevated to the Sacred College of Cardinals at the next consistory. At the same time he mentioned that Tedeschini had been named cardinal *in pectore* (known only to the Pope) on March 13, 1933. The appointment had been kept secret because official anticlericalism was rife in the spring of 1933 during the debates on the Law of Religious Congregations and Denominations.

The whole affair of the negotiations for a concordat ended on a rather ludicrous note, which somehow summed up official relations between Spain and the Holy See. In December, Alcalá Zamora in a glittering ceremony placed the cardinal's biretta upon Tedeschini's head. The president of one of the most laic and anticlerical republics in the world, in honoring the nuncio of the Holy See, was following a tradition reserved for those nations with whom the Holy See enjoyed good relations.

iv

While the Cortes was in recess during the late summer of 1934, Gil Robles decided that it was time for the CEDA to secure some ministerial positions. He felt that he had proved his republicanism to the Spanish people. Furthermore, the Radicals were on the verge of moral bankruptcy and had long since lost all popular support; if he did not do something soon, the president would be forced to call new elections.

The Socialists and many of the left republicans announced that they would not stand for the admission of the CEDA to the ministry. They were convinced that Gil Robles intended to overthrow the republic; at the very least they felt his party would complete the moral disintegration of the republic. In looking abroad the left found a deadly parallel. In Austria, Catholic Chancellor Engle-

October Revolution

bert Dollfuss had suspended the Austrian constitution
and had openly attacked the Austrian Socialists. Gil
Robles had visited Dollfuss shortly after the event, and
the Spanish Socialists were convinced that he intended to
follow the Austrian leader's pattern.[16] The left threatened, warning of violence if the CEDA joined the ministry.

When the Cortes reconvened on October 1, 1934, the
CEDA refused to vote confidence in the Radical ministry
and Gil Robles demanded that three *cedistas* be admitted
to a new ministry. Consultations followed, but the president had no choice; Alcalá Zamora did not want new elections at this time. He charged Lerroux with forming a
ministry including the three: Rafael Aizpún as minister
of justice, José Anguera de Sojo as minister of labor, and
Manuel Jiménez Fernández as minister of agriculture. In
these selections, Gil Robles offered three of his most moderate followers; Jiménez Fernández particularly was a true
friend of the working man.

The left found its warnings ignored and it responded
with a general strike by the UGT and armed uprisings
in Madrid, Barcelona, and the Asturian mining region.[17]
In Madrid, the revolt was quickly put down although the
city was paralyzed by the strike for a week. In Barcelona,
the Esquerra declared the independence of the Catalan
state within the Spanish Federal Republic, but the revolt
miscarried because the CNT did not support the uprising

16. Gil Robles stated that he had no such intentions. He and Dollfuss were Catholic leaders and their main enemy, in both cases, was the
Socialists, but the political situation in Austria was quite different from
that of Spain. Gil Robles was well aware that a suspension of the Spanish constitution would provoke immediate civil war. (Interview with
José María Gil Robles, Madrid, April 22, 1960.)

17. The UGT demanded the acceptance of a radical ten-point program. Point four called for the dissolution of all the religious orders,
confiscation of all their property, and the expulsion of the Jesuits from
Spain. Ramos-Oliviera, *Politics, Economics and Men*, pp. 507-8.

there. There was violence, nonetheless, and in some Catalan towns churches were burned and priests were assaulted. Similar outbreaks occurred in La Coruña, Valencia, and León, but all were put down. The most serious struggle developed in the Asturias and centered around the towns of Oviedo and Gijón.

The Asturian miners displayed a rare solidarity. All of the working class organizations—the UGT, the CNT, and the small Communist groups—joined in a common front and marched on Oviedo and Gijón. The army garrisons and the civil guard in those towns took refuge in a few strongholds while waiting for reinforcements from Madrid.

The fighting was as violent as only a civil war can be and most of Oviedo was destroyed. There were atrocities on both sides: the miners burned churches and killed priests; when the government troops—Moorish soldiers commanded by General Francisco Franco—arrived, their reprisals were just as violent. Some ten thousand casualties were reported.

The church's losses were great: thirty-seven clergy were killed and fifty-eight churches were burned or destroyed. Some of the clergy had been clearly murdered, having given no provocation; ten Christian Brothers and six seminarians in Oviedo were among this number. The Cathedral of Oviedo, used as a garrison by the government troops, was destroyed, along with many of the buildings of the University of Oviedo.[18]

After the fighting had ended, the fate of the revolutionaries became the main political issue in the nation. The prisons were crowded with leftists. Azaña was arrested for treason, but he later proved his innocence; he had gone to Barcelona, not to join in the revolt, but rather

18. Montero Moreno, *Persecución religiosa*, pp. 41-52.

to warn against it. The extreme right demanded the death penalty for the revolutionaries (although the constitution outlawed capital punishment), and the army began trying the leading conspirators, sentencing many to death under military law. The cases were sent to the council of ministers for review.

Alcalá Zamora, mindful of the pardon given the Sanjurjo conspirators, wanted the sentences commuted to life imprisonment. Gil Robles was faced with a dilemma: if the CEDA voted for death, such an outcry would be raised that the ministry might topple; if it voted against the death penalty, Gil Robles felt that this would reveal a weakness in time of crisis. The episcopate did not back the extreme right. Cardinal Vidal y Barraquer asked the government's clemency for the revolutionaries. The Archbishop of Burgos, although denouncing the killing of the clergy, forgave the revolutionaries for their acts, admitting that "it is no secret that the working classes in the industrial and mining areas have deserted the Church."[19]

The ministry finally compromised. Two revolutionaries who had committed common crimes were sentenced to death, but most of the conspirators were granted clemency. Nonetheless, the prisons still bulged with anarchists, many of whom used the new-found time to read Bakunin and Marx for the first time in their lives. The ministry survived the crisis. However, Gil Robles used the issue for political ends as more cases came up for review. He achieved many of his demands, all of which, he felt, brought him closer to his goal, the premiership.

The October revolution was important. The CEDA increased its strength by using the issue to appeal to the moderates. The monarchists continued to plot with the

19. *Boletín Oficial Eclesiástico del Arzobispado de Burgos,* October 25, 1934, pp. 263-66.

army to overthrow the republic, for they realized that there was no chance of their coming to power without bloodshed; if the left had revolted because three moderate *cedistas* had been admitted to the ministry, a royalist victory at the polls would surely precipitate civil war.

The loss of the rebellion was a setback for the left extremists, but they learned a valuable lesson—that of uniting for victory. The miners had been effective where the rebels of Madrid and Barcelona had not because Asturians of all leftist shades—Socialists, anarchists, and Communists—had united. The left was to apply this lesson a year later to achieve victory at the polls.

If anything, the revolution underscored the enormity of the social problem, for the repeal and nonimplementation of the social reforms of the Republican-Socialists had served to goad the proletariat to revolt.

v

As Gil Robles pressed towards his goal of becoming premier, his party lost all sense of social reform. In May, 1935, he withdrew support from the Lerroux ministry because it would not go along with his demands for the death penalty for twenty-one of the imprisoned miners. A new ministry was formed, still led by Lerroux, but with Gil Robles as minister of war, along with four other *cedistas* and two Agrarians. In the shuffle a true reformer lost his post; Jiménez Fernández was dismissed from the ministry of agriculture.

Jiménez Fernández had been a veritable thorn in the oligarchy's flesh. He was dedicated to social reform. Even the leftist reformers recognized in him a kindred soul. As Ramos-Oliviera commented later, "A Spanish conservative and a Catholic with common sense would be bound to achieve rare notoriety."[20] During his seven months' tenure he had introduced numerous reform bills (urgently needed because the effects of the depression were creating widespread unemployment), but he ran headlong into the power of the landowners and the right extremists. The Traditionalist leader, José Lamamié de Clairac, excoriated Jiménez Fernández' reforms on the floor of the Cortes. Although his party supported him on many issues, his leader, Gil Robles, commented that Jiménez Fernández was unwise in condemning all of the landowners (many of whom had dismissed their laborers and let their lands go uncultivated simply to spite the republican reforms) because many had not recovered from the "terrible experience of the revolution," and many others did comply with their duty.[21] As Jiménez Fernández saw many of his reforms perverted he gave up hope, and when he was dismissed in 1935, all hope of social reform went with him.

However, some of the bishops became active proponents of social reform. Bishop Múgica, for example, urged the faithful of Vitoria to help out all unemployed workers —even the Communists, Socialists, and anarchists.[22] After the October revolution, the Bishop of Oviedo invited the workers of that strife-torn region to return to the church, and he established a commission to study the social problem in his diocese.

For Gil Robles, reform was no longer an important goal; obtaining the premiership was his obsession. Should it not rightly belong to him, as leader of the largest party in the Cortes? One man—the president—stood in his way.

Alcalá Zamora's dislike of the *cedista* leader was primarily personal. He had no use for the young man who

20. *Politics, Economics and Men*, p. 520.
21. *C.E.D.A. Organo de la Confederación Española de Derechas Autónomas*, December, 1934, p. 2.
22. *Boletín . . . Vitoria*, June 1, 1934, pp. 367-80.

had risen so spectacunely and opportunely. To the president, Gil Robles represented the clerical right, that group which had never forgiven Alcalá Zamora for his anticlericalism. Then, there was the question of Gil Robles' republicanism—admittedly opportunistic (and perhaps the president saw a younger likeness of himself here). Could the president trust Gil Robles to maintain the republic if he were appointed premier? Would not there be another revolution as in 1934? These questions had personal implications; the vain Alcalá Zamora basked in his role as president of the republic. He did not want to lose his job, which he would certainly place in jeopardy if an appointment of Gil Robles met with dissension and a demand for new elections. According to the constitution, he was allowed to dissolve the Cortes only once without having to answer for it. Alcalá Zamora knew that he would never survive another election; both right and left detested him and were waiting eagerly to depose him. He could count only on the support of the Radicals, and he spent most of 1935 trying to breathe new life into that party. But, Gil Robles as premier? Never!

The question of Gil Robles' republicanism was and is a frequently debated subject. Certainly he was an opportunist, for he would have supported any government that safeguarded the church's rights. However, he was opposed to violence, and there are indications that by 1935 he had completely accepted the republic. Gil Robles had three opportunities with success assured to overthrow the republic. He took none of them. After the October revolution, he could have effected a coup with probable success; in May, 1935, he could have overthrown the government, as he controlled the ministry of war and the army; finally, he could have supported General Manuel Goded's plans in February, 1936. (See Chapter 13.)

But, he did not believe that a dictatorship would solve Spain's problems. Although his speeches often hinted of violence, there were few who judged the man by his deeds and not by his words.

By mid-summer of 1935, Gil Robles gave up his hopes for the premiership and turned to his original scheme—the project for constitutional revision. He secured presidential approval of his outline and a parliamentary commission was appointed to study it. His plan maintained the separation clause of Article 3, but called for a revision of Articles 26 and 27 repealing the laws against the religious orders (including the Jesuits), allowing complete freedom of education, and providing for a concordat with the Holy See.[23] December, 1935, was the target date, for revisional amendments could legally be submitted then. He stated that his party would collaborate with any government to effect constitutional revision.[24]

This last plea indicated that the CEDA was rapidly losing support, which indeed it was. The monarchist-inclined *cedistas* had begun to desert. The Basque Nationalists who had supported him earlier were now completely alienated, because their autonomy petition had been turned down (illegally, it is important to add). Even the Pope declared that the church was not united to any political party, a point he had insisted upon all along, but which had special meaning, coming at this time;[25] Gil Robles' political stock with the Vatican was declining. The younger *cedistas* were weary of the government's inaction and the lack of social reform; many drifted to the Falange. Gil Robles attempted to bolster his party by drawing closer to the center and coming to an agreement with the Radicals. At a meeting in Salamanca in June,

23. *El Debate*, June 23, 1935.
24. *A.B.C.*, August 15, 1935.
25. *El Debate*, May 10, 1935.

1935, Gil Robles praised Lerroux and announced that "we have seen the Republic as a means of saving Spain, and we unite with you [Lerroux] in a cordial embrace."[26]

All to no avail. CEDA's majority cabinet fell in September when the Agrarians withdrew confidence; they were wary of whom Gil Robles would embrace next—even Azaña, they thought, if the liberal leader would support revision of the religious laws. Joaquín Chapaprieta formed a Radical ministry that lasted until December 15, under an aura of financial scandals involving illegal gambling and a game of musical chairs within the ministry to ensure almost everyone in the Radical party a life-long pension for having held a ministerial post. When Chapaprieta fell, Alcalá Zamora still declined to appoint Gil Robles as premier, and the *cedistas* then refused to support any other ministry. Thereupon, Alcalá Zamora had no choice. He appointed Manuel Portela Valladares, a Radical, as interim premier, dissolved the Cortes, and announced elections for a new Cortes to be held on February 16, 1936.

To what extent was Gil Robles responsible for the *bienio negro?* Although he held more power than any other politician during these two years, he did not enjoy absolute power (or nearly the amount held by Azaña during the 1931-33 period). But there is little doubt that his campaign commitments to the oligarchy diminished his reform plans considerably. He had a reason—the political salvation of the Spanish church—and he realized this aim, but at the expense of the country.

Given the circumstances, it would not be farfetched to argue that a wiser politician would have forgotten the religious laws. For in actuality, the church was being allowed to function without too much interference. True,

26. *Ibid.*, June 25, 1935.

the religious laws were on the books, but the left had hanged itself politically in 1933 trying to enact them. The CEDA made the same mistake trying to effect their repeal. The CEDA's insistence upon a first preference for the legal restoration of the church's rights without at the same time offering a sensible nonreligious political program was as imprudent a policy as was the left's insistence that the religious laws be carried out to the letter. Vigorous social reform was the nation's crying need, and only this action could have consolidated the republic with the masses as no other action could. Essentially, both the right's and left's concern with the religious problem took up sorely needed time and effort that could have been applied constructively to the social problem. The religious question, for both, was divisive, because it was not Spain's most important problem. Gil Robles' clericalism was no more effective a solution to the republic's political problems than was the left's anticlericalism. In both instances, the religious problem was used to cement coalitions that should have been based on more realistic approaches. The attitudes of both groups were to prove fatal, not only for their respective political programs, but for the republic as well.

CHAPTER 13

THE POPULAR FRONT
AND THE CHURCH

i

When the president dissolved the Cortes in December, 1935, and called elections for February 16, 1936, an undeclared civil war began in Spain. In the four and a half years since the proclamation of the republic few problems had been solved; indeed, greater problems had come into being. As a result, issues were more sharply defined, and moderate Spaniards began to drift to extreme positions. On the right, Renovación Española and the Falange attracted many *cedistas*; while on the left, anarcho-syndicalist and Socialist strength grew. In the face of this polarization to extremes, Spain faced the most important elections in almost a century.

Because of the political problems of the *bienio negro*, the right had lost its cohesiveness, while the left now showed a strong tendency towards union. On January 15, 1936, all of the forces of the left announced their union into one electoral coalition, the Popular Front. This union included Left Republicans, Socialists, Radical Socialists, and Communists. The anarcho-syndicalists, true to their ideals, did not participate in the union (except for Ángel Pestaña, one of their leaders), but it was apparent that most of them intended to vote for the Popular Front because the Popular Front made an important electoral promise—a general amnesty for political prisoners. The prisons were full of anarcho-syndicalists mainly as a result of both the October revolution of 1934 and the countless acts of industrial violence since 1933.

Announcing its formation, the Popular Front promised political amnesty and "full implementation of the Constitution."[1] It did not mention religion or the church, but there was no doubt that it intended to implement the religious laws if elected. That the Popular Front would do so with a vengeance seemed certain, because of the *bienio negro* government's inactivity on this matter.

In the face of the Popular Front, the right felt the pressure to unite, for under the Spanish electoral law, division could only prove fatal. Could the right unite?

The disunion of the right, apparent since the elections of 1933, had become exacerbated by 1936. The monarchists had no use for the CEDA or for the republic. Indeed, their disdain for the CEDA almost exceeded their hatred for the republic. The Traditionalists placed no hope in victory through union. They had already given up the legal struggle. The *requetés* continued to drill as the party secretary, Manuel Fal Conde, traveled throughout Navarre preaching armed insurrection. They would have nothing to do with the CEDA and accused it of perverting the aims of Acción Católica. Their organ noted: "In accordance with the wishes of the Pope, we respect Acción

1. *El Mundo Obrero* (Madrid), January 16, 1936.

Católica. . . . We are watchful that it does not become a political party. But, disgracefully, it is a great influence in Acción Popular, which party takes advantage of the faithful."[2]

José Calvo Sotelo, the leader of Renovación Española, was more conciliatory. He invited Gil Robles to join the Bloque Nacional, a coalition of nonrepublicans whose aim was to restore the monarchy. The Bloque, he said, must proclaim Spain to be Catholic, "because even apart from other reasons, Catholicism . . . was a decisive and determining factor in our nationality."[3] Gil Robles refused. Stinging from the rebuff, Calvo Sotelo attacked the CEDA-Radical pact of July, 1935, as being an ideological impossibility, that of the "Catholic faith with an incredulous positivism."[4]

Gil Robles could absorb the monarchists' rebukes for he felt victory within his grasp. If the *bienio negro* had proved anything, it had proved his republicanism; furthermore, he was strongly allied with the Radicals now. All he had to do was win a few more seats in the Cortes and a CEDA-Radical coalition could be assured of a parliamentary majority. However, he had to be careful, because his pact with the Radicals was already alienating some of the clericals in the CEDA's ranks. He also had to be wary of the Popular Front's strength.

Gil Robles tried to resurrect the old right coalition of 1933. The formation of the Popular Front provided the needed impetus. However, although right coalitions were formed throughout Spain, there was no single national union. Different groups made up the right coalition: in Madrid it was the CEDA, Renovación Española, and the

2. Galindo Herrero, *Los partidos monárquicos*, p. 165.
3. *Ibid.*, p. 127.
4. *Ibid.*, p. 131.

Radicals; in the northern provinces it was the CEDA, Renovación Española, and the Traditionalists. It was difficult to keep this coalition together, for in some provinces the monarchists refused to ally with either the CEDA or the Radicals. Thus, on a national scale the right coalition included such diverse groups as the anticlerical Radicals and the theocratic Traditionalists. It was, of course, no more ludicrous than the Popular Front's diversity—bourgeois republicans and Soviet-directed Communists working in unison.

Understandably, the right could not agree on a political manifesto other than being "anti-Marxist." Gil Robles stated that a manifesto was unnecessary;[5] he should have admitted that one was impossible. Furthermore, the Catholic front was broken, as the Basque Nationalists refused to run with either coalition.

The episcopate had much at stake in the elections and the bishops used all of their resources to prevent a Popular Front victory. The Popular Front was clearly anticlerical, and the thought of thousands of anarcho-syndicalists freed from prison was enough to frighten any cleric. Therefore, in marked contrast to the 1933 elections, the episcopate circulated pastorals opposing the Popular Front.

Cardinal Gomá, just returned from the consistory in Rome, issued a pastoral with near-papal authority. The primate said the Pope had advised that "in the face of the union of the forces of irreligion, the rightists have to unify in defense of religion." Gomá declared that although the church did not oppose the diversity of partisan politics, a Catholic's first obligation was to "vote for the candidate pledged to safeguard the rights of God in society." Was the church hindering the use of political liberty? No, said

5. *A.B.C.*, January 24, 1936.

the cardinal. The church desired free political choice for all citizens, but this liberty was limited because "spiritual goods are . . . higher than temporal ones," and a person's obligations to God were more important than his obligations to his fellow man. "The rights of man," he declared, "should never exclude the rights of God . . . nor should purely political interests ever precede religious ones." Clearly, this was an appeal to vote for the right.[6]

Many of the other bishops joined their primate in issuing pastorals—the bishops of Ávila, Córdoba, Málaga, and the Cardinal Archbishop of Seville—but the Bishop of Barcelona put the church's concern in the clearest terms. He warned that "upon the coming elections . . . can depend the existence of Catholic Spain."[7] His observation so infuriated the Catalan anticlericals that an Esquerra leader responded with a threat to kill the bishop for his "political meddling."[8]

The campaign was intense, but it produced nothing new in electoral propaganda. The right's press devoted itself to listing all of the church burnings and social disorders of the previous five years. Both Calvo Sotelo and Gil Robles made constitutional revision their primary issue. The Popular Front candidates said little about religion—they had found the promise of amnesty a more binding issue than anticlericalism.

All parties felt certain of victory, and none more so than the new party organized by the president and the interim premier, Portela Valladares. The two had formed a party, the "Centre," appealing to the Radicals; essentially, theirs was a Radical party without Lerroux. Through official manipulation, Alcalá Zamora hoped to secure a majority for his Centre party.

6. *Boletín . . . Toledo,* January 15, 1936, pp. 33-47.
7. *El Debate,* January 17, 1936.
8. *Ibid.,* January 26, 1936.

Enthusiastically then, the parties presented their lists to the voters on February 16. The Popular Front carried the nation with a popular vote of 4,176,156; the forces of the right had 3,783,601; and the center polled 681,047.[9]

Under the electoral system the makeup of the new Cortes was: Popular Front, 256; right, 143; and the center, 54. After the Cortes investigated charges of corruption at the polls, it revised the seating to 278 for the Popular Front, 134 for the right, and 55 for the center. In this final adjustment the Socialists had the largest number of deputies (allotted by a pre-electoral agreement among the leaders of the Popular Front) with 99 and the Left Republicans had 87. With 88 deputies, the CEDA was the largest party on the right and the second largest in the Cortes. Portela Valladares' 16 Centrists led the center. Lerroux was not re-elected; his Radicals won only four seats.[10]

Apparently, the Popular Front won because of the strength of its union and popular dissatisfaction with the *bienio negro*. The popular vote was close. Considering the voting strength of the anarcho-syndicalists, it would not be farfetched to say that they were a decisive factor in the Popular Front's success at the polls. And now, the anarcho-syndicalists wanted something for their support.

ii

The election results came as a great shock to the right; it had been so certain of victory. The postelection letdown was intense and many *cedistas* simply gave up the parliamentary struggle and turned to more promising methods of ensuring religious peace. If a voice in the

9. Hugh Thomas, *The Spanish Civil War* (New York, 1961), p. 94, agrees with most sources, more or less; no official statistics were ever issued. The Basque Nationalists had 130,000 votes and are not counted with either right, left, or center.

10. *Ibid.*, p. 93.

Cortes could win them nothing, then perhaps the sword could. Their leader however, did not share their feelings.

Gil Robles was entirely opposed to an illegal plan to nullify the election results. Although he was approached by leading members of the army and the monarchists to support their scheme to prevent the Popular Front leaders from coming to power—in effect to overthrow the legal basis of the republic—he refused.[11] He had accepted the democratic framework of the republic, despite all of his 1933 campaign speeches, and he was convinced that more harm than good would come from any illegal attempt to thwart the mandate of 1936. If the church was to live once again in peace it could not do so by hiding behind the army's sword.

Premier Portela Valladares was also approached. General Francisco Franco urged him to declare martial law and turn over power to the army, which would then maintain Portela in the ministry. The premier refused. Rebuffed, the generals and the monarchists retired to make longer-range plans.

Two days after the elections, Portela Valladares, now fearful of violence, resigned his ministry. Alcalá Zamora called in Manuel Azaña to head a Popular Front ministry. Upon taking office, the new premier announced that his ministry would work within the law and that no person had reason to fear persecution.[12]

Why should a premier have been obliged to state the obvious—that his ministry would work within the law? The nature of the governing coalition made such a statement necessary. For, the victory of the Popular Front, so promising in its reform implications, ultimately proved disastrous. The essence of its union made implicit a power

---

11. See Buckley, *Spanish Republic*, p. 195.
12. *A.B.C.*, February 21, 1936.

struggle within the government. Azaña was beholden to the anarcho-syndicalists for his victory, but the political and social programs of the Left Republicans and the anarcho-syndicalists were as antithetic as those of the moderate leftists and the Traditionalists; at least, the Traditionalists believed in government. Furthermore, prisons were being opened throughout the country—wardens were not even waiting for orders from Madrid. As thousands of anarcho-syndicalists were released, they immediately turned to violent attacks upon the right. They did so with impunity, knowing that Azaña's ministry remained in power only through their support. The main object of their attack was the Falange. The members of the Falange did not shrink from political brawl'ng and they matched the anarcho-syndicalists blow for blow, confident that every act of retaliatory violence would reflect upon the government. Throughout Spain, gangs of *pistoleros* roamed the streets as the Falange and the FAI (Federación Anarquista Ibérica, the hard core organization of the anarcho-syndicalists) carried out a personal feud.

To add to Azaña's worries, the Popular Front coalition began breaking apart. The rift between republicans and Socialists had never been healed since the first falling out in 1933. Some moderate Socialists grouped around Indalecio Prieto in giving complete support to Azaña, but Francisco Largo Caballero moved most of the Socialists to the extreme left. He founded a newspaper, *Claridad,* which virtually preached revolution, and by the beginning of the summer he was sharing the same speaking platform with the Communists.[13] He took the Socialist youth organization over with him.

13. The Communists had been allotted sixteen seats in the Cortes for their participation in the Popular Front's victory. See David T. Cattell, *Communism and the Spanish Civil War* (Berkeley, 1955), p. 31.

On the right, Renovación Española stood clearly outside of the republic. Its monthly, *Acción Española,* noted that "we are . . . the disciples of Cardinal Cisneros [the sixteenth century cleric] who placed the defense of his just cause in the force of cannons. To these . . . and not to ballot boxes we confide . . . the supreme interests of religion and fatherland."[14] The Falange began to attract more followers as many moderates became convinced that the republic was a lost cause. In April, Ramón Serrano Suñer, the leader of the CEDA youth organization, Juventudes de Acción Popular, deserted Gil Robles and took the group over to join the Falange. At the same time, the generals, Francisco Franco, José Sanjurjo, Emilio Mola, and Manuel Goded, were planning a coup for late October.

This was the situation Spain faced in the spring of 1936. It was civil war on a small scale, with the government powerless to do anything. Besides having to cope with these problems, the government had to continue to provide normal services, to legislate, and above all, to deal with an aggravated agrarian problem. Normal social and economic problems would have been difficult enough without the violence of the political situation.

In May, the situation was further worsened when the Cortes deposed Alcalá Zamora from the presidency and elected Manuel Azaña to that office. Alcalá Zamora's departure was a cause of rejoicing for all parties, but Azaña's leaving the premiership was a great loss. He was the one man whom the entire left supported and trusted; he was their most able leader. In this time of crisis he was elected to occupy a largely powerless office. Although he took the office mainly because he was determined never to let the Socialists form a ministry, his per-

14. Galindo Herrero, *Los partidos monárquicos,* p. 152.

sonal administrative ability and power were wasted in the presidential office.

Santiago Cesares Quiroga, a Galician republican, took over the premiership. If the government had been ineffective under Azaña before May, it floundered now. There appeared no hope for Spain.

iii

Almost immediately after the Popular Front government took over, there was a new and violent wave of church burnings. Throughout Spain, churches were fired, and the government made few attempts to stop the destruction. In addition, the headquarters of Acción Popular in many towns were also attacked and destroyed.

These burnings followed no set pattern but most evidence points to anarchist responsibility. The anarchists were determined now, more than ever, to implement the proletarian revolution, and what could be more in accord with their tradition than the burning of churches? Furthermore, it appears that the anarchists were abetted by common criminals, who had also been released in the wholesale opening of prisons after the elections. The government could do nothing to protect the churches for it needed the support of these extremists. Occasionally, the civil guard was posted near some of the churches, generally with little success. In some of the northern towns Carlist *requetés* stood guard over the churches.

An interesting example of a church burning during this period was the destruction of the parish church of San Luis in Madrid, during the second week in March. Although the church was only some two hundred yards from the office of the home ministry, the government took no action to restrain or apprehend the burners. The newspapers, forbidden by the censor to describe the burnings, said nothing; *El Liberal* simply opined that *falangistas* had secretly fired the church in an effort to turn Catholic sentiment against the republic.[15] The primate protested to the premier and asked protection for church property. Azaña replied that "the Church's rights as recognized by the law of the State will be respected and protected."[16] Azaña was grasping for an order that no longer existed.

On April 15, social disorders were discussed in the Cortes. Calvo Sotelo claimed that in the two-month period since the elections, 36 churches had been completely destroyed and 106 had been partially damaged.[17] To these charges, Rodolfo Llopis, a Socialist, answered that church burning was a Spanish tradition. The church had always taken sides against the workers, he said, and the church had lost its neutral position because "each pulpit and confessional had been a campaign headquarters against the Popular Front. . . . We would like the religious problem to be one of conscience, but if the Church is going to play politics, it is going to get hurt."[18] Ángel Pestaña, the only anarcho-syndicalist in the Cortes, declared that people burned the churches because "they have always seen the priest as a parasite and enemy of the working classes."[19]

When Azaña took the floor to answer the charges against his ministry, he decried the disorders and urged all to keep calm, claiming that the government could still handle any problems of the public order with confidence.[20]

Perhaps the inability to live up to these claims per-

15. March 15, 1936.
16. *Boletín . . . Toledo,* April 1, 1936, p. 151.
17. *CDE,* April 15, 1936, pp. 47-58.
18. *Ibid.,* p. 31.
19. *Ibid.,* p. 45.
20. *Ibid.,* April 16, 1936, p. 5.

suaded Azaña to leave the premier's office. Shortly before he was elected president, an incident occurred which hearkened back a century to the time when the Jesuits had been accused of poisoning the wells. On May 4, in Madrid, a child was reported ill after having eaten candy given it by a woman wearing a nun's habit. The rumor spread that the candy was poisoned and was part of a church plot to kill the working-class children. Irate mothers attacked the woman, seriously injuring her, and extremists used the occasion to claim that nuns were distributing poison everywhere; as a result, three churches, four religious schools, and one *convento* were assaulted and burned. The following day the home minister, Casares Quiroga, stated that his investigations had proved that the child involved was in good health and that the rumors had been entirely false. He blamed the affair on extremists.[21]

The disorders continued under Azaña's successor. Calvo Sotelo presented a new list to the Cortes on May 6. From April 1 to May 4, he claimed, fifty-three churches had been burned and ninety-nine had been partially destroyed.[22] On June 16, Gil Robles stated that thirty-six churches had been totally destroyed and thirty-four had been sacked during the month-long period from May 13 to June 15. The grand total since February, he claimed, was 160 churches totally destroyed and 251 partially ruined.[23] The left never questioned the validity of these figures.

In addition to this violence, the church faced the threat of implementation of the religious laws, one of the Popular Front's implied electoral promises. The Popular Front was determined to execute the legislation.

21. *El Socialista*, May 5, 1936, and *Claridad* (Madrid), May 4, 1936.
22. *CDE*, May 6, 1936, p. 27.
23. *Ibid.*, June 16, 1936, pp. 14-16.

Two weeks after the election, Francisco Barnés, the minister of public instruction, announced a plan for the substitution of the religious orders in teaching. He ordered the primary school inspectors to survey the school system to determine which institutions could replace the regular clergy immediately. He stated that he wanted the substitution in Madrid to take place as quickly as possible.[24]

The church was powerless to stop him, and the minister began to act as soon as the survey was completed. In Viscaya, a Catholic teachers' association was ordered to disband. In Santander, a primary school run by nuns was closed, despite the civil governor's protest that the children had no other means of education available. By mid-May, the plan was in full operation and the closing of religious schools in various localities all over Spain was announced.

In the Cortes, the right questioned the minister's actions and attacked the closings on two counts: that the government was not providing adequate substitution, and that arbitrary closing of religious schools violated the Law of Religious Denominations and Congregations (the law did allow religious schools as long as they were not operated by the religious orders). Barnés answered that the law was on the books and was going to be enforced. He and Llopis argued that the right was to blame for any hardships suffered, for it had had two years in which to provide effective substitution machinery and had done nothing.[25]

As more schools were closed, *El Debate* published statistics from the Madrid *ayuntamiento* to show that there were 27,202 students in religious schools, and 61,910

24. *El Sol*, March 1, 1936.
25. *CDE*, June 3, 1936, p. 48.

children not attending school in Madrid. It claimed Barnés had no place to educate these children.[26] The minister continued to close schools. Under the circumstances, no impartial observer could call his actions less than spiteful, for Barnés was wrecking the entire educational system in his zeal to enforce the religious laws.

The religious orders were also dismissed from other civil duties. Early in March, the Sisters of Charity were expelled from the administration of a home for aged people in Alcalá de Henares. In Alcory, the clergy were given fifteen days to vacate two churches, which were ordered to be converted into a school and market place. In Barcelona, Madrid, and Segovia, nuns in charge of asylums and hospitals were ordered to leave.

The government also decreed the reorganization of the Jesuit expropriation commission and ordered the quick and thorough confiscation of Jesuit property. In the Cortes, the Socialists introduced a bill to end clerical pensions, but the republicans did not support the bill, and it failed to pass.

Thus, for the first time since 1931, the church was faced with massive implementation of the religious legislation. The teaching provision of the laws touched the church's most sensitive spot. In this position, it would have supported any group that could have effectively protected it.

iv

The church could not stay neutral. It became more than ever politically allied with the right. At the same time, it could not offer substantial aid to the right, for it was the weakest link; the church burnings and religious legislation proved that it could be attacked so much more

26. June 2, 1936.

easily than any other institution. Its position became fixed, mainly as a result of the left's attacks and the right's support.

In this moment of crisis, the church's internal weaknesses were apparent. Cardinal Gomá commented on this in a circular of March 1. He observed that many of the faithful were on the verge of losing their faith as a result of the press campaign against the church, neopaganism, and poor teaching by the clergy. The primate ordered the clergy to avoid scandal by staying out of the streets and cafes and to be more modest in dress and conversation. He commanded them to stay "completely out of . . . political life" and to be courteous and attentive to the civil authorities.[27]

The Holy See was also disturbed by the Popular Front's victory and the ensuing violence against the church. Two weeks after the election, *L'Osservatore Romano* warned Catholics that they should be prepared to see the government drift to the extreme left, and the Pope commented in early April that "sad moments had . . . arrived for Spain."[28]

In all of this turbulence, two persons who had played prominent roles in the politico-religious history of the previous fifteen years left Spain. Ángel Herrera Oria resigned the presidency of Acción Católica and departed to Switzerland to enter a seminary to study for the priesthood. Cardinal Tedeschini also left Spain in early June.

Tedeschini's recall to Rome was a normal occurrence, for a cardinal rarely serves as nuncio. His departure prompted sadness among moderate leftists. *El Sol* praised the cardinal for his moderating influence upon the Catholic monarchists and for his general attitude toward the

27. *Boletín . . . Toledo,* March 1, 1936, p. 93.
28. *El Debate,* April 2, 1936.

republic.[29] Monsignor Felipe Cortesi, formerly nuncio to Argentina and Paraguay, was appointed to the Madrid post.

The Spanish government also changed ambassadors. It accepted Pita Romero's resignation and, on April 10, appointed Luis de Zulueta, the diplomat to whom the Holy See had refused a *placet* in 1931, as ambassador to the Holy See. This time Zulueta was accepted promptly, and one month later he presented his credentials to the Pope. Why the change? Probably, the Holy See wanted a diplomatic representative from the republic at any cost; the situation was too tense, and there was no room for bargaining now as there had been in 1931. In 1936 the Holy See could not afford the attitude of 1931.

In any event, the Holy See's policy was now entirely passive. The Popular Front government would have to stabilize itself and adopt a permanent religious policy before the Holy See could initiate a discussion of church-state relations. Furthermore, the Holy See could no longer rely on the CEDA to protect the church.

If the episcopate and the Holy See had lost confidence in political parties, the decline of the CEDA was their reason. Now that the church needed protection the CEDA was unable to rally the right to a legal defense of the church. In 1933 it had tried to be all things to all men; now it lacked the support of even moderate rightists. Only a hard core of party regulars remained, for the monarchists and *falangistas* now formed the nucleus of the right.

Gil Robles had tried to maintain his confidence after the elections. Believing that a moderate solution for Spain's problems was still possible, he stated his support for the republic and said that he planned to form a new

29. June 2, 1936.

party composed of the center and right moderates.[30] In the same mood, he declared three weeks later that the CEDA was the only stronghold of the right and that, when the Popular Front government had run its course, the CEDA as a center-right party would be ready to take over and provide stable government for the nation.[31]

Events, however, precluded any possible hope in the CEDA as a solution to Spain's political ills. The polarization of the nation into extremist camps led to mass desertion from the moderate parties; there was no longer any room for a center. After Serrano Suñer took the CEDA's youth organization over to the Falange, Gil Robles lost hope in his party. In May, he was a tired man who declared that he was considering leaving political life because so many of his *cedistas* were becoming Fascists.[32]

v

The Spain of July, 1936, found no place for the men of moderate views, the men the country needed so desperately. Azaña found himself in a powerless office, Gil Robles was left without followers, and Prieto could count on only a minority of the Socialists. The extremists, however, were gaining both power and support. Largo Caballero kept drifting farther left, attacking the moderates, calling for the proletarian revolution, and glorying in the title of "the Spanish Lenin." On the right, despite the imprisonment of Primo de Rivera, the Falange continued its violent ways.

There were rumors of coups. The Comitern, it was said, had made plans to take over the government later in the year. Many Spaniards heard that the army, in con-

30. *El Sol*, February 18, 1936.
31. *El Debate*, March 6, 1936.
32. *La Vanguardia* (Barcelona), May 6, 1936.

junction with the monarchists, was planning to rise against
the republic in October. Most people felt that it was only
a question of time before the republic would fall to
plotters.

On July 13, the event occurred which precipitated
open struggle between the extremists. On that day, Calvo
Sotelo was assassinated by a group of assault guards in
retaliation for the murder of one of their number a few
days earlier by the Falange. All moderate Spaniards were
shocked by this event. The army decided to take advantage of the moderates' mood, and it advanced the planned
date for its coup. On July 17, the garrisons in Africa revolted against the republic, and the following day the pen-
insular garrisons arose. In the north, the Carlist *requetés*
proclaimed against the republic. Most of the right quickly
joined with the army, which expected to attain complete
victory within a matter of days. The government, however, consolidated its position and strength. The Spanish
Civil War had begun.

CHAPTER 14

HEREDITARY HISTORY

The Spanish Civil War came to serve as a focal point for all the brewing discontents of two centuries of Spanish history. It was the predictable outcome of the polarization of political, economic, and social life. The war also brought the politico-religious problem to a climax, although the problem still remains; in fact, it appears to be endemic to Spanish history. In this regard, some generalizations concerning the nature of the Spanish church and its conflicts with the state can profitably be made as conclusions to this study.

In Spain, as in every country, church-state relations have not been as primarily conditioned by the legal status of the church within the state as they have been by the amount of power and influence the church has had upon the body politic and the social fabric of the nation. The fact of establishment or separation per se has had little to do with the presence or absence of the church's political power. In essence, all nations have similar politico-religious problems, which vary in intensity as the power of all the institutions of a nation vary. Moreover, the relationship of institutions within a country are important. Specifically, the Spanish church's political power derived from the nature of the Spanish state and the historical character of the Spanish people. Thus, if Spain had had a sound tradition of political and intellectual freedom, supported by the force of the state, the Spanish church would have exhibited this same soundness and love of liberty. This tradition was lacking, and both church and state had encroached upon the other's domain; both had been found wanting in that inner compelling force that is the basis of free institutions.

The Roman Catholic church, as an institution, has preserved its ability to adapt to and absorb the characteristics and traditions of each country. While maintaining the universality of dogma necessary to an international institution, the church, as a national institution, has come to differ within each nation as nations differ from each other. Furthermore, it should not be overlooked that the Spanish clergy are Spaniards; and the truism that the clergy are no different from the people certainly is true in Spain as elsewhere. If the Spanish church has shown a history of authoritarianism, intolerance, and imperviousness to change, it is because the Spanish church has been composed of Spaniards who, throughout their history, have also tended to authoritarianism, intolerance, and imperviousness to change.

The Spanish church has always been a politically conservative institution. Its support of conservative governments had been conditioned in part by the knowledge that it has survived in Spain for over fifteen centuries. Governments of all forms have come and gone, but the

church has remained. Therefore, the church has preferred those governments which have promised it a
privileged position and which have guaranteed order and
domestic stability within the country. In conflicts with
radically progressive governments, the church has, not
unwillingly, awaited the support of the conservatives; and
these latter, in turn, have often used the church to further
their political ambitions.

Above all, the spiritual strength of the Spanish church
—always an incalculable—cannot be underestimated. Despite the apostasy of the working classes and the loss of
the intellectuals, it has always been able to count on the
support of a large section of the middle and upper classes.
In times of stress, the church has been able to attract
many more supporters to its position.

If one criticism could be made of the leaders of the
reformist parties, the clergy, and the moderate Catholic
party, it would be that they all had—in varying degrees—
an incomplete grasp of the realities of Spain in the 1930's.

Specifically, the reformers apparently felt that the
church was the main threat to the stability of the republic
and that they could eliminate that threat through legislation. In reality, the extreme monarchists and the anarchists were much greater threats to the republic. Had the
reformers treated the church with moderation, they
would have assured themselves of clerical support, or at
least neutrality. The price of the clerical budget and the
cost of maintaining troops to protect the churches from
extremists would have been a small price to pay for the
church's support. Furthermore, the reformers failed to
take advantage of the division within the church by appealing to the moderate Catholic party. Had they made
an effort to absorb the moderate Catholics into the reformist parties, they would have taken an important step

toward stabilizing the republic against extremists. The bonds of social reform would have been much stronger than the tenuous ties of anticlericalism. The reformers made a serious mistake in considering the republic as a closed club, open only to anticlericals.

The clergy, likewise, made serious errors of judgment. They were aware of the antireligion and anticlericalism of the reformers and they should have realized that Múgica's and Segura's pastorals in April and May, 1931, would lead to violence. The clergy allied themselves too strongly with the reactionary parties. The clergy's support of their pro-church policies was reasonable, but there was no reason why the clergy had to give wholehearted support to the rest of the reactionaries' programs. The moderate Catholic party made two serious mistakes: the CEDA's reliance upon the monarchists effectively negated its claims to being a republican party, and its insistence upon repealing the religious legislation without offering a workable and reasonable social program did it more harm than good.

The ultimate consequences of this struggle were disastrous. The reformers, by exaggerating the religious problem, lost the support of the moderates and were unable to effect all of their reforms. The clergy did not take the opportunity to purge themselves of unworthy elements and to end their reliance upon the reactionary political and social groups. As a result, the republican experiment failed, and Spain suffered not only the bloodshed of the Civil War but also the establishment of a privileged-class dictatorship, which by 1964 has ruled Spain for a quarter of a century.

Perhaps Manuel Azaña put his finger on the key to modern Spanish history in a speech he delivered in 1930, during the early days of the republican movement. Spaniards, he said, had to be emancipated from their past because it had ruined their present. "Just as there are persons who suffer from hereditary diseases," he remarked, "so Spain, as a country, suffers from 'hereditary history.'"[1]

1. Speech of November 20, 1930, cited in Joaquín Arrarás Iribarren, *Historia de la cruzada española* (Madrid, 1940), I, 226.

BIBLIOGRAPHY

PRIMARY SOURCES

PUBLIC DOCUMENTS

Spain. *Boletín oficial del ministerio del estado.* 1930-36.
——. *Boletín oficial del ministerio de justicia.* 1930-36.
——. *Boletín oficial del ministerio de instrucción pública y bellas artes.* 1930-36.
——. Las Cortes Españolas. *Congreso de los diputados: Extracto oficial.* 1934-36.
——. Las Cortes Españolas. *Diario de las sesiones de las Cortes: Congreso de los diputados.* 1933-34.
——. Las Cortes Españolas. *Diario de las sesiones de las cortes constituyentes de la república española.* 1931-33.

CHURCH CATECHISMS, ENCYCLICALS, PASTORALS, SERMONS

García Mazo, Santiago José. *El catecismo de la doctrina cristiana.* 36th ed. Valladolid: Talleres Tip. "Cuesta," 1924.
Gomá y Tomás, Isidro Cardenal. *Antilaicismo.* 2 vols. Barcelona: Rafael Casulleras, Editor, 1935.

——. *Pastorales de la guerra de España*. Estudio preliminar de Santiago Galindo Herrero. Madrid: Ediciones Rialp, S.A., 1955.

Guisasola y Menéndez, Victoriano. *La acción social del clero*. Valencia: M. Gimens, 1910.

——. *Justicia y caridad en la organización cristiana del trabajo*. Madrid: Imp. Asilo de Huérfanos de S.C. de Jesús, 1916.

Jover Balague, José. *Los heraldos de paz, desde mi púlpito*. Madrid: Suc. de F. Peña Cruz, 1931.

Maura y Gelabert, Juan. *La cuestión social*. Madrid: Imp. de Ricardo Rojas, 1902.

Martínez Núñez, P. Zacarías, O.S.A. *Discursos y oraciones sagradas*. 2nd ed. El Escorial: Imp. de Real Monasterio, 1929.

Martínez de Ripalda, Jerónimo, S.J. *El catecismo de la doctrina cristiana*. 40th ed. Madrid: Edit. Apostolado de la Prensa, S.A., 1934.

Pius XI. *Ad catholici sacerdotii*. Rome: December 20, 1935.

——. *Dilectissima nobis*. Rome: June 3, 1933.

Pla y Deniel, Enrique. *Despojo persecutorio de la iglesia o separación económica del estado?* Alegato Dirigido al Excmo. Sr. Ministro de Justicia ante la Supresión del Culto y Clero. Ávila: Imp. Católica, 1931.

Reig y Casanova, Enrique. *Presente y porvenir económico de la iglesia en España*. Madrid: Tip. de la Revista de Archivos, Bibliotecas, y Museos, 1908.

——. *La acción social católica en España*. Madrid: Tip. de la Revista de Archivos, Bibliotecas y Museos, 1924.

Tedeschini, Federico Cardenal. *Discursos y cartas sobre acción católica española*. ed. J.D.F. Santiago de Compostela: Imp. Paredes, 1958.

SPEECHES

Albornoz, Álvaro de. *La política religiosa de la república*. Madrid: Tip. de S. Quemades, 1935.

Azaña, Manuel. *Discursos en campo abierto*. Madrid: Espasa-Calpe, S.A., 1936.

——. *En el poder y en la oposición (1932-1934)*. 2 vols. Madrid: Espasa-Calpe, S.A., 1934.

————. *Una política, 1930-1932.* Madrid: Espasa-Calpe, S.A., 1932.

Herrera Oria, Ángel. *La posición de la derecha española en la política actual.* Discurso Pronunciado . . . en el Teatro Apolo de Valencia, December 21, 1931. Madrid: Editorial Ibérica, 1932.

Pildáin y Zapiáin, Antonio. *En defensa de la iglesia y la libertad de enseñanza.* Discursos en las Cortes Constituyentes y Conferencia en el Monumental Cinema. Madrid: Ediciones FAX, 1936.

Gil Robles, José María. *Discurso pronunciado . . . en la asamblea de las juventudes de acción popular celebrada en Covadonga el día 9 de Septiembre de 1934.* Madrid: Imp. Palomenque, 1934.

MEMOIRS

Aguirre, José Antonio de. *Entre la libertad y la revolución, 1930-1935.* Bilbao: Imp. Verdes Achirica, 1935.

Arrese, Domingo de. *El país vasco y las constituyentes de la segunda república.* Madrid: Gráficas Modelo, 1932.

Bowers, Claude G. *My Mission to Spain: Watching the Rehearsal for World War II.* New York: Simon and Schuster, 1954.

Buckley, Henry W. *Life and Death of the Spanish Republic.* London: H. Hamilton, 1940.

Castrillo Santos, Juan. *Cuatro años de experiencia republicana, 1931-1935.* Madrid: Gráfica Administrativa, 1935.

Domingo, Marcelino. *La escuela en la república: La obra de ocho meses.* Madrid: Bolaños y Aguilar, 1932.

————. *La experiencia del poder.* Madrid: Tip. de S. Quemades, 1934.

Gil Robles, José María. *Spain in Chains.* New York: America Press, 1937.

Gordón Ordás, Felix. *Una campaña parlementaria: El articulo 26 de la constitución y los háberes pasivos del clero.* Madrid: Imp. de G. Sáez, 1934.

Lerroux, Alejandro. *La pequeña historia: Apuntes para la historia grande vividos y redactados por el autor.* Buenos Aires: Editorial Cimera, 1945.

Lizarza Iribarren, Antonio. *Memorias de la conspiración: Como se preparó en Navarra la cruzada, 1931-1936.* Pamplona: Editorial Gómez, 1953.

Mendizábal, Alfredo. *The Martyrdom of Spain: Origins of a Civil War.* Translated by C. H. Lumley, with an introduction by Jacques Maritain. New York: Charles Scribner's Sons, 1938.

Ossorio y Gallardo, Ángel. *La España de mi vida.* Buenos Aires: Editorial Losada, S. A., 1941.

Palau, P. Gabriel, S.J. (ed.). *Diario íntimo de un cura español (1919-1931).* Barcelona: Herederos de Juan Gili, 1932.

Shaw, Rafael. *Spain From Within.* London: T. Fisher Unwin, 1910.

Vila, Enrique. *Un año de república en Sevilla.* Seville: La Editorial Sevillana, S.A., 1932.

ECCLESIASTICAL BULLETINS

Boletín oficial eclesiástico del arzobispado de Burgos. 1931-36.
Boletín oficial eclesiástico del arzobispado de Sevilla. 1931-36.
Boletín oficial eclesiástico del arzobispado de Toledo. 1931-36.
Boletín oficial eclesiástico del arzobispado de Zaragoza. 1931-36.
Boletín eclesiástico de la diócesis de Ávila. 1931-36.
Boletín oficial eclesiástico del obispado de Córdoba. 1931-36.
Boletín oficial del obispado de León. 1931-36.
Boletín eclesiástico del obispado de Madrid-Alcalá. 1931-36.
Boletín oficial del obispado de Orense. 1931-36.
Boletín oficial del obispado de Salamanca. 1931-36.
Boletín eclesiástico del obispado de Vitoria. 1931-36.

NEWSPAPERS

Spanish
A.B.C. (Madrid), 1931-36.
Ahora (Madrid), 1931-36.
Arriba. (Madrid), 1935-36.
CNT (Madrid), 1933.
Claridad (Madrid), 1936.

El Debate (Madrid), 1931-36.
Frente Rojo (Madrid), 1932.
La Gaceta de Madrid, 1931-36.
La Gaceta del Norte (Bilbao), 1931-36.
La Gaceta Regional (Salamanca), 1933.
El Imparcial (Madrid), 1931-36.
Informaciones (Madrid), 1931-36.
El Liberal (Madrid), 1931-36.
El Liberal (Seville), 1931-36.
El Mundo Obrero (Madrid), 1931-36.
La Nación (Madrid), 1931-36.
Opinión (Barcelona), 1933-36.
El Siglo Futuro (Madrid), 1931-36.
El Socialista (Madrid), 1931-36.
El Sol (Madrid), 1931-36.
Solidaridad Obrera (Barcelona), 1935-36.
La Tierra (Madrid), 1931-36.
La Vanguardia (Barcelona), 1931-36.
Voz de Guipúzcoa (San Sebastián), 1933-35.

Foreign

The New York Times, 1931-37.
L'Osservatore Romano (Vatican City), 1931-36.
The Times (London), 1931-36.

PERIODICALS

Acción Española (Madrid), 1932-36.
Bulletin of Spanish Studies (London), 1931-36.
C.E.D.A. Organo de la Confederación Española de Derechas Autónomas (Madrid), 1934-35.
Ciencia Tomista (Madrid), 1931-36.
Cruz y Raya (Madrid), 1933-35.
Cruzada Católica (Madrid), 1932-35.
Fray Lazo (Madrid), 1931-32.
Gracia y Justicia (Madrid), 1931-32.
Razón y Fe (Madrid), 1931-36.
Religión y Cultura (Madrid), 1931-36.
Revista Eclesiástica (Madrid), 1931-36.

GENERAL WORKS

Anuario eclesiástico de España. Barcelona: Editorial Pontífica, 1931-34.

Anuario de educación y enseñanza católica de España. Madrid: Ediciones FAX, 1935.

Anuario estadístico de España. Madrid: Sucesores de Rivadeneyra, S.A., 1930-34.

Aznar, Severino. *El catolicismo social en España: Nuestro primero curso social*. Vol. II. Zaragoza: Mariano Escar, 1906.

Azpiazu, P. Joaquín, S.J. *La acción social del sacerdote*. Madrid: Biblioteca Fomento Social, Ediciones FAX, 1934.

Castro Albarrán, Aniceto de. *El derecho a la rebeldía*. Madrid: Imp. Gráfica Universal, 1934.

Chica, José M. de la. *Las luchas políticas: Como se incendiaron los conventos en Madrid*. Madrid: Editorial Castro, S.A., 1931 (?).

Codigos y leyes españoles: Legislación española, leyes religiosas. Madrid: J. Mª· Yagues, ed., 1935.

El concordato de 1851. Madrid: Sección de Asuntos Eclesiásticos del Ministerio de Justicia, 1921.

Feliz, Victoriano. *La conquista de la juventud obrera*. Madrid: Editorial Razón y Fe, 1935.

———. *Jóvenes campesinos de acción católica y social*. Madrid: Editorial Razón y Fe, 1934.

Gil Robles y Quiñones, José María. *El derecho y el estado y el estado de derecho*. Salamanca: Imp. Editorial Salmantina, S.A., 1922.

Hervás, Juan. *La Acción católica y la política*. Madrid: Sáez Hnos., 1936.

Jiménez de Asúa, Luis. *Proceso histórico de la constitución de la república española*. Madrid: Editorial Reus, S.A., 1932.

Llopis, Rodolfo. *Hacia una escuela más humana*. Madrid: Editorial Espana, 1934.

López Núñez, Álvaro. *Inventorio bibliográfico del grupo de la democracia cristiana*. Vol. I. Obras Originales. Madrid: Imp. de Antonio Marzo, 1925.

Manterola, José de. *La disolución en España de la compañía de Jesus, ante sus consecuencias, el sentido común, y el derecho.* Barcelona: M. Carbonell, 1934.

La Monarquía: El Rey Alfonso XIII ante S.S. Pío XI. Una fecha histórica en el catolicismo mundial. Madrid: Imp. de A. Marzo, 1925.

Monge y Bernal, José. *Acción popular: Estudio de biología política.* Madrid: Imp. Sáez Hnos., 1936.

Nevares, Sisinio, S.J. *El Porqué de la sindicación obrera católica.* Madrid: Editorial Razón y Fe, 1930.

Nievas, Cipriano. *En torno a la república española.* Madrid: Luz y Vida, 1933.

Peiró, P. Francisco. *El problema religioso-social de España.* 2nd ed. Madrid: Editorial Razón y Fe, 1936.

Pérez Serrano, Nicolás. *La constitución española: Antecedentes, texto, comentarios.* Madrid: Editorial Revista de Derecho Privado, 1932.

Tarquini [pseud]. *El anteproyecto de la constitución del estado: Herejías de la comisión jurídica asesora y refutación de todas ellas.* Valladolid: Imp. Casa Social Católica, 1931.

Torrubiano Ripoll, Jaime. *Beatería y religión: Meditaciones de un canonista.* Madrid: Ediciones Morata, 1930.

———. *La iglesia rica y el clero pobre.* Madrid: Imp. Artistica, 1922.

———. *Política religiosa de la democracia española.* Madrid: Sucesores de Rivadeneyra, S.A., 1933.

———. *Rebeldías: El gran problema religioso en España.* Vol. II. Madrid: Editorial Minerva, 1926.

Vegas Latapié, Eugenio. *Catolicismo y república.* Madrid: Gráfica Universal, 1932.

Vicent, P. Antonio, S.J. *Cooperatismo católico: Cooperativas de consumo, de crédito, y de producción.* Valencia: Imp. de José Ortega, 1905.

Yaben, Hilario. *Monarquía o república?* Madrid: Alamaque Popular de Cultura Religiosa, 1931.

ARTICLES

Aizpún, P. L. "Hemos fracasado?" *Revista Ecclesiástica*, 56 (April, 1936), 361-72.

Azpiazu, P. Joaquín, S.J. "El salario familiar y las cajas de compensación," *Razón y Fe*, 442 (November, 1933), 336-57.

Izaga, P. Luis, S.J. "La iglesia, el régimen político, y los partidos," *Razón y Fe*, 429 (October, 1932), 199-211.

——. "La iglesia y las vicisitudes políticas de los pueblos," *Razón y Fe*, 412-13 (June 10, 1931), 289-307.

——. "A las puertas del vaticano," *Razón y Fe*, 455 (December, 1934), 433-49.

——. "La situación jurídica de los religiosos en España," *Razón y Fe*, 414 (July 10, 1931), 5-25.

Llopis, Rodolfo. "Las ordenes religiosas siguen explotando la enseñanza en la república española," *Leviatán*, 3 (July, 1934), 59-63.

Marina, M. "La última lección: Comentario electoral," *Razón y Fe*, 471 (April, 1936), 433-51.

Molina Muñoz, P.R. "La falta de clero y de obras postelescolares en Andalucía," *Razón y Fe*, 466 (November, 1935), 325-35.

Montavan, William F. "The New Spanish Republic," *Commonweal*, XV (March 9, 1932), 513-15.

Piux XI, "Dilectissima nobis," *Razón y Fe*, 438 (July, 1933), 291-99.

"La última crísis política en España," *Razón y Fe*, 408 (March 25, 1931), 536-53.

Vargas Zúñiga, P.E. "El problema religioso de Espana," *Razón y Fe*, 462-63 (July-August, 1935), 289-307; 465 (October, 1935), 145-64; 468 (January, 1936), 99-116.

Vélez, P.M., "La revolución y la contrarevolución en España," *Religión y Cultura*, 98 (February, 1936), 195-235.

OTHER SOURCES

United States State Department Dispatches from Spain and Italy (unpublished). Washington, 1931-36.

Personal interview with José María Gil Robles, Madrid, April 22, 1960.

Personal interview with Dr. Ángel Herrera Oria, Bishop of Málaga, Madrid, April 8, 1960.

SECONDARY SOURCES

GENERAL WORKS

Alessandrini, Federico. *La Spagna e la reppublica, 1931-1936.* Rome: Editrice A.V.E., 1945.

Alcalá Galiano, Álvaro. *La caída de un trono (1931).* Madrid: Compañía Ibero-Americano de Publicaciones, S.A., 1933.

Altamira y Crevea, Rafael, and Zabala y Lera, Pío. *Historia de España y de la civilización española.* Vols. IV, V. Barcelona: Suc. de Juan Gili, 1911, 1930.

Antequera, José María. *La desamortización eclesiástica considerada en sus diferentes aspectos y relaciones.* Madrid: Imp. de A. Pérez Dubrull, 1885.

Araujo García, C., and Grubb, Kenneth G. *Religion in the Republic of Spain.* London: World Dominion Press, 1933.

Arrabal, Juan. *J. M.ª· Gil Robles: Su vida, su actuación, sus ideas.* Madrid: Imp. Sáez Hnos., 1933.

Arrarás Iribarren, Joaquín. *Historia de la cruzada española.* Vols. I, II. Madrid: Edicones Españoles, 1940.

——. *Historia de la segunda república española.* Vol. I. Madrid: Editora Nacional, 1956.

Aznar, Severino. *La revolución española y las vocaciones eclesiásticas.* Madrid: Instituto de Estudios Políticos, 1949.

Ballesteros y Beretta, Antonio. *Historia de España y su influencia en la historia universal.* Vols. VII, VIII, IX. Barcelona: Salvat Editores, S.A., 1941.

Becker, Jerónimo. *Relaciones diplomáticas entre España y la Santa Sede durante el siglo XIX.* Madrid: Imp. de Jaime Ratés Martín, 1908.

Blanco Nájera, Francisco. *Antijuricidad de la ley sobre secularización de cementerios.* Barcelona: Edit. Casals, 1932.

Borkenau, Franz. *The Spanish Cockpit: An Eyewitness Account of the Political and Social Conflicts of the Spanish Civil War.* London: Faber and Faber, Ltd., 1937.

Brenan, Gerald. *The Spanish Labyrinth: An Account of the Social and Political Background of the Civil War.* 2nd ed. Cambridge: The University Press, 1950.

Buitrago y Hernández, Joaquín. *Las órdenes religiosas y los religiosas en España*. Madrid: Tip. á cargo de D. Adolfo R. de Castroviejo, 1901.

Burgos y Mazo, Manuel de. *El problema social y la. democracia cristiana*. 6 vols. Barcelona: Luis Gili, 1914-30.

Canals, Salvador. *La caída de la monarquía, problemas de la república, instalación de un régimen*. Madrid: Ruíz Hnos., 1931.

Castillejo y Duarte, José. *War of Ideas in Spain: Philosophy, Politics, and Education*. London: J. Murray, 1937.

Cattell, David T. *Communism and the Spanish Civil War*. Berkeley and Los Angeles: University of California Press, 1955.

Chapman, Charles E. *A History of Spain*. New York: The Macmillan Co., 1938.

Cortés Cavanillas, Julián. *Gil Robles monárquico? Misterios de una política*. Madrid: Librería San Martín, 1935.

Díaz, José Simón. *Cien fichas sobre la iglesia católica durante la segunda república (1931-1939)*. Madrid: I.N.L.E., 1958.

Díaz del Moral, J. *Historia de las agitaciones campesinos andaluzas*. Cordoba, Madrid: Revista de Derecho Público, 1929.

Díez del Corral, Luis. *El liberalismo doctrinario*. Madrid: Instituto de Estudios Políticos, 1945.

Enciclopedia universal ilustrada. Bilbao: Espasa-Calpe, S.A., 1923——.

Episodios de la revolución en Asturias: Los pasionistas de Mieres (Asturias) y la revolución de octubre de 1934, episodios narrados por los mismos protagonistas. Santander: El Pasionario, 1935.

Epstein, M. (ed). *The Statesman's Yearbook*. London: Macmillan and Co., 1931-36.

Fernández Almagro, Melchor. *Historia del reinado de Alfonso XIII*. Barcelona: Juan Gili, 1933.

——. *Historia. de la república española, 1931-1936*. Madrid: Biblioteca Nueva, 1940.

Galindo Herrero, Santiago. *Breve historia del tradicionalismo español*. Madrid: Publicaciones Españolas, 1956.

——. *Los partidos monárquicos bajo la. segunda república*. Madrid: Ediciones Rialp, S.A., 1956.

García y García de Castro, Rafael. *Las apologistas españoles (1830-1930).* Madrid: Ediciones FAX, 1935.

——. *Los intelectuales y la iglesia.* Burgos: Imp. Aldecoa, 1934.

García Venero, Maximiano. *Historia del nacionalismo vasco, 1793-1936.* Madrid: Editora Nacional [Uguina], 1945.

Germain, André. *La Révolution espagnole en vingt-cinq tableaux.* Paris: B. Grasset, 1931.

Iturralde, [P.] Juan de. *El catolicismo y la cruzada de Franco.* Vol. I. Vienne: Editorial Egui-Indarra, 1955.

Jobit, Abbé Pierre. *Les Éducateurs de l'Espagne moderne.* Paris: Bibliothèque de l'École de Hautes Études Hispaniques, Vol. XIX, 1936.

Laín Entralgo, Pedro. *España como problema.* Vol. II: *Desde la "generación del '98" hasta 1936.* Madrid: Aguilar, 1956.

López Morillas, Juan. *El Krausismo español: Perfil de una aventura intelectual.* México, Buenos Aires: Fondo de Cultura Económica, 1956.

Madariaga, Salvador de. *Anarquía o jerarquía: Ideario para la constitución de la 3ª república española.* Madrid: Aguilar, 1935.

——. *Spain: A Modern History.* New York: Frederick A. Praeger, 1958.

Los mártires de Turón: Notas biográficas y reseña del martirio de los religiosos barbaramente asesinados por los revolucionarios en Turón (Asturias), el 9 de octubre de 1934. Madrid: La Instrucción Popular, 1935.

Manuel, Frank E. *The Politics of Modern Spain.* New York: McGraw-Hill Book Co., 1938.

Marvaud, Ángel. *L'Espagne au XXᵉ siècle.* Paris: Librairie, Armand Colin, 1913.

——. *La Question sociale en Espagne.* Paris: Félix Alcan, Editeur, 1910.

Menéndez y Pelayo, Marcelino. *Historia de los heterodoxos españoles.* Madrid: Victoriano Suárez, 1930-44.

Moody, Joseph N. (ed.). *Church and Society: Catholic Social and Political Thought and Movements, 1789-1950.* New York: Arts, Inc., 1953.

Montero Moreno, Antonio. *Historia de la persecución religiosa en España, 1931-1935.* Madrid: La Editorial Católica, 1961.

Morote, Luis. *Los frailes en España.* Madrid: Imp. de Fortanet, 1904.

Mourret, Fernando. *Historia general de la iglesia.* Vol. IX, Part II: *La iglesia contemporánea.* Translated by P. Bernardo de Echalar. Madrid: Editorial Voluntad, 1937.

Núñez, Ignacio. *La revolución de octubre de 1934.* 2 vols. Barcelona: Ed. José Vilamela, 1935.

Payne, Stanley G. *Falange: A History of Spanish Fascism.* Stanford: Stanford University Press, 1961.

Peers, E. Allison. *Spain, the Church and the Orders.* London: Eyre and Spottiswoode, 1939.

———. *The Spanish Tragedy, 1930-1935: Dictatorship, Republic, Chaos.* New York: Oxford University Press, 1936.

Pla, J. *Historia de la segunda república española.* 4 vols. Barcelona: Destino, 1940.

Ramos-Oliviera, Antonio. *On the Eve of Civil War in Spain.* London, 1937.

———. *Politics, Economics, and Men of Modern Spain, 1808-1945.* Translated by Teener Hall. London: Victor Gollancz, Ltd., 1946.

Reid, John T. *Modern Spain and Liberalism.* Stanford: Stanford University Press, 1937.

Requejo San Román, Jesús. *El Cardenal Segura.* Madrid: Imp. Juan Bravo, 3, n.d.

Rucabado, Ramón. *Los mártires de Asturias. La escuela mártir de Turón.* Barcelona: Catalunya Social, 1935.

Shiels, W. Eugene, S.J. *King and Church: The Rise and Fall of the Patronato Real.* Chicago: Loyola University Press, 1961.

Smith, Rhea Marsh. *The Day of the Liberals in Spain.* Philadelphia: University of Pennsylvania Press, 1938.

Solana y Gutiérrez, Mateo. *Miguel Maura y la disolución de las órdenes religiosas en la constitución española.* Mexico: Imp. Cooperativa Mexicana, 1934.

Soto de Gongoiti, Juan. *Relaciones de la iglesia católica y el estado español.* Madrid: Inst. Editorial Reus, 1940.

———. *La Santa Sede y la iglesia católica en España.* Madrid:

Publicaciones de la Comisión de Legislación Extranjera e Información Jurídica, 1942.

Thomas, Hugh. *The Spanish Civil War.* New York: Harper & Brothers, 1961.

Tovar González, Laureano. *Ensayo biográfico del Excmo. Senor Cardenal Ilundáin y Esteban.* Pamplona: Editorial Aramburu, 1942.

Trend, John B. *The Origins of Modern Spain.* Cambridge: University Press, 1934.

Valle, Florentino del, S.J. *El P. Antonio Vicent, S.J. y la acción social católica española.* Madrid: Editorial Bibliográfica Española, 1947.

Vicens Vives, J. *Historia social y económica de España y América.* Vol. V. Barcelona: Editorial Teide, 1959.

Wright, John J., Bishop of Worcester, Mass. *National Patriotism in Papal Teaching.* Westminster, Md.: The Newman Press, 1956.

ARTICLES

Burks, R. V. "Catholic Parties in Latin Europe," *Journal of Modern History,* XXIV, No. 3 (September, 1952), 268-86.

Cuneo, Dardo. "Fernando de los Ríos y el socialismo humanista," *Cuadernos Americanos,* LXXVIII (November-December, 1954), 85-113.

García Villoslada, P. Ricardo, S.J. "La iglesia y el estado en España y Portugal," in Montalbán, Francisco J., S.J. *Historia de la iglesia católica.* Vol IV: *Edad moderna (1648-1951).* Madrid: Biblioteca de Autores Cristianos, 1951, pp. 522-83.

Jackson, Gabriel. "The Azaña Regime in Perspective (Spain, 1931-1933)," *American Historical Review,* LXIV, No. 2, (January, 1959), 282-300.

———. "The Origins of Spanish Anarchism," *Southwestern Social Science Quarterly,* XXXVI (September, 1955), 135-47.

Madden, Marie R. "Status of the Church and Catholic Action in Contemporary Spain," *Catholic Historical Review,* XVIII, No. 1 (April, 1932), 19-59.

Shapiro, J. Salwyn. "Anticlericalism," *Encyclopedia of the Social Sciences.* New York: Macmillan Co., 1931, pp. 112-14.

INDEX